THE ACTOR'S
OTHER
SELVES

THE ACTOR'S OTHER SELVES

Subpersonalities as a Major Acting Approach

ERIC MORRIS

ERMOR ENTERPRISES

Edited by Carin Galsett

Published by
Ermor Enterprises
8004 Fareholm Drive
Los Angeles, CA 90046

ISBN: 978-0-9836299-8-6

This book is dedicated to the memory of Hal Stone, PhD, who left us in May of 2020. He was my teacher and friend. My journey with Hal and his wife, Sidra, who was also his partner in their work, was life changing. Their work and the many books that they wrote together impacted the lives of thousands of people. They were pathfinders and innovators exploring subpersonalities as a life-altering process. They encouraged all of us to elevate our consciousness and to achieve happiness. I will forever be grateful to both of them for taking me on that journey which opened up so many doors for me. I will miss him always and hold him in my heart.

Sidra too is a PhD. She is very much alive and will hopefully continue the legacy that she and Hal created.

CONTENTS

INTRODUCTION

My personal journey with subpersonalities started forty years ago. I had not even heard the word before that. I discovered the concept quite by accident and as the result of a recommendation from one of the actors who was training with me. I had been in psychotherapy for about eight years, struggling with a difficult marriage. The therapy I was in was not really helping me to make any changes in the relationship, so my student asked me why I was continuing to see the psychologist I was working with if in fact nothing was changing. It was a very good question, especially since I had already devoted eight years of my life to that therapy. She suggested that I see Doctor Hal Stone, a psychologist who had been very helpful to her and who practiced short-term therapy. I called him and made an appointment to see him. A PhD psychologist, like his wife Sidra, he was working from his home in

North Hollywood, while she had an office on Ventura Boulevard. They had been working with subpersonalities, based on C.G. Jung's archetypes, and they were using a technique called *voice dialogue,* a two-person process involving a facilitator and a person being facilitated. The purpose for using that technique was to make the facilitated person discover and become conscious of what subpersonalities were present and how they functioned in his life and to establish what is called an *aware ego.*

I parked my car in front of a very nice California ranch-type house, a single-level house type that is very indigenous to the Los Angeles area. I hesitantly pushed the doorbell button and waited for someone to open the front door. I was filled with fear and suspicion, thinking that this might be one of those California "woogie" fads that promised miraculous results. At that point in time I had never heard about subpersonalities, and the description that my student had given me had only increased my anxiety. The most important thing that she had told me, though, was that it was a short-term process; and after having struggled for eight years in group and one-on-one therapy, I was really ready for the prospect of successful help, which is why I had decided to explore it.

Hal greeted me at the front door, smiled and ushered me into what looked like a sunroom directly off the living room. He was a little above average height, past middle age with rosy cheeks and a shock of thick salt-and-pepper hair. The room was small, with two places where to sit, a chair and a stool next to it. Hal sat on what looked like a two-pillow loveseat facing the chair and the stool. I sat in the chair, waiting for him to say something. He sat there in silence for what seemed like a very long moment, looking at me and obviously trying to pick up whatever he could before saying, "So tell me, why are you here?" I told him that I was having a great deal of trouble in my marriage and no success dealing with the problems in the therapy I was involved in, at which point he broke in and asked me to move over and sit on the stool, because he wanted to hear that voice that I had just shared with him. For a long moment I just stared at him, thinking, What the hell did I just get into at $150 an hour? He repeated his request: "OK, let me talk to that part of you." Wow! OK, I thought, I'm here so I'm going to humor him. I adjusted myself on the stool, as he began to talk to me, asking questions that I really don't remember, but in an instant all hell broke loose. I was instantly filled with an anger that expressed itself at the top of the vocal register. I screamed, began to cry, and continued to purge from a place that I hadn't known existed, even though I had been an actor for many years and was used to large theatrical expurgations in a wide variety of human emotional areas. Hal moved me back and forth between the chair and the stool, speaking to a variety of my "other selves." By the time the session was over, I had been blown away by the experience!

That was when this forty-year journey began. I started working with Hal and a group of eight people in his living room on a very large couch. He would facilitate one person at a time using VOICE DIALOGUE as the approach. He would speak to various parts of each person's other selves, moving people over physically a foot or two from one voice to the next. The group consisted mostly of professionals—psychologists, teachers, doctors, and so on. There were three actors in the group, including me. We met twice a week, mostly facilitated by Hal, and ultimately we began to do voice dialogue with each other. I was there consistently for about two years. We also worked with our dreams and how they influence our life. Dreams and dreaming are a very important part of our life, and what we learn and experience from them is life changing. I am going to devote a great deal of information to that subject.

It was in my very first session with Hal that I realized what an incredible tool subpersonalities could be for actors. And with some adjustments I began to use voice dialogue in my classes with great success in liberating actors from the multitude of blocks and obstacles that kept them from being free to act. I did that for several months before abandoning voice dialogue as an instrumental-therapy exercise in my classes. I was already dealing with trying to overcome a reputation for practicing psychotherapy without a license. In reality that was not at all what I was doing. My work, my process, and my approach to the training of actors include the psychology involved in instrumentally liberating them from their lifelong fears, obstacles and emotional blocks. Over the sixty years I have been teaching acting, I have had many psychiatrists, psychologists, and other mental-help professionals work with me for long periods of time. Many of them have said that they use a lot of my techniques in their practices. I still do voice dialogue as an instrumental exercise but only in workshops I call jamborees, three- or four-day intensive workshops we have in the mountains, where at times the entire emphasis is on subpersonalities.

I have already written a lot about this subject in four of my other books, and I will use some of the same material in this book, because most people who are attracted to this book will not have read or are not interested in perusing those other volumes. In this book I am going to demystify what subpersonalities are, making the material simpler, more understandable and applicable. It has taken on a kind of supernatural quality and I believe has been misinterpreted and misused. The mysticism surrounding it has complicated a process that can be more easily understood and applied. There is a plethora of books, articles, and treatises on subpersonalities, but as far as I know there aren't any specifically written for actors and directors.

CHAPTER 1

CONSCIOUSNESS

Ignorance is the greatest human disease! The largest number of people on the planet Earth have it, and it is deadly! Because of it, we have experienced wars, plagues, terrorism, racism, and religious holocausts. For years I have said to the people in my classes that the journey from birth to death is for the elevation of consciousness. Becoming conscious is not a gift; it is something to be worked for and accomplished.

THE COMPONENTS OF CONSCIOUSNESS

AWARENESS

Most people walk around as if in a fog, totally oblivious to their surroundings. Curiosity is most often expressed in fulfilling creature needs, in questions such as: What am I going to have for lunch, or where should I go? I wonder if I have any texts or emails. Is it going to rain today? I can't remember: did it rain yesterday? Gee, when did they turn this street into a one-way boulevard? If you asked people to close their eyes and describe the room they have been living in for years, they would most likely not be able to be specific about the objects there. Most people accept things without any awareness of the realities or consequences of their actions and habits. They continue eating animals, for example, even though the proven results from a lifetime of doing so are heart disease, hypertension, clogged arteries, pandemics, and a long list of digestive ailments. They have blind faith in organized religion without asking any questions about the efficacy of God. From the beginning of time religion has caused more death and destruction than any other force in our world: It has been responsible for the Crusades, the Inquisition, the burning of people accused of being witches, jihads, holocausts, and genocides. When will mankind become aware, conscious of what reality is: finding your loving self and elevating awareness of the differences in people and the undeniable similarities between us?

The actor must practice achieving awareness on a daily basis, looking and seeing everything in every environment. When you walk into a room, activate all of your senses. Listen to the sounds—everything you hear coming from outside and the ambient sounds of the room itself. Notice the odors. How many different ones do you detect? Where are the sounds and odors coming from? What are the colors of the walls and the floor, and how many objects occupy the space? What does the furniture look like—its colors, shapes, sizes? Sensorially speculate on how the texture of the objects and the fabric feel to your tactile sense, and do the same with outdoor environments. We are gifted with five senses. Learn to challenge them, employ them, excite them. To achieve a high level of awareness in life is life changing and mandatory for the artist.

CURIOSITY

I was blessed with curiosity. It was a great asset to my life, since I was curious about everything! It was, however, a liability in grade school and even in high school. I would ask the teachers about the things they were explaining and would encounter frustration as a response to my questions. "Fred (my original name before I changed it)," they would reply, "why is it important for you to know that? Does it make a difference in what I am explaining?" I thought it did and was very often frustrated that most of the time I received no answers to my queries.

My curiosity is a wonderful gift. It allows me to explore and learn about so many things and people. It leads me into fantasies that become the entertainment and joys of my life. Once, in an exercise I was doing with him, an actor in my class, who seemed very ignorant about the questions I was asking him, got angry and decided to challenge my knowledge about almost everything, except acting and what we were doing. "OK, Eric," he asked, "what do you know about airplanes and rockets?" at which point I spent more than five minutes expertly responding to him. He went on with a barrage of questions on a variety of subjects, and I was able to respond positively. I explained that I knew a lot about some things and a little about a lot of things. I do not know everything and do not claim to.

Curiosity is a very important component for becoming conscious. It leads to journeys and explorations most people never embark on. Elevating your curiosity goes far beyond a suggested assignment. It is a journey into the abyss! Almost everything an actor does to evolve and grow as a person is part of the training we are involved with. To repeat a statement that I have made hundreds of times: *An actor is an actor twenty-four hours a day, seven days a week, four weeks a month, twelve months a year for life.* There is nothing that an actor should not be interested in.

Children have an almost inborn curiosity about everything. Daddy, they ask, why do birds fly? Where do babies come from? And so on. Unfortunately that inborn curiosity is very soon discouraged, and children become aware of how impatient their parents get when they ask all of those questions, so they stop asking and too soon their curiosity atrophies. We as actors must elevate our *threshold of interest;* we must find ways to appeal to our curiosity. Ask questions about everything! Start by finding the things that interest you and encourage yourself to wonder about them. Those things will dovetail into other interests and curiosities. Continue on a daily basis to ask questions of everything and everybody. We take so many things for granted, and because of that we become jaded. I have a great deal of knowledge about the human body, about illnesses, treatment, medicine, nutrition, vitamins—what they do and how they work in the body. I love automobiles and have an encyclopedic knowledge of cars. I know about guns and firearms—classic, historic and modern—about art, painting, great artists and their lives, artistic periods and styles. The list is endless. I am using my own experiences to communicate that the knowledge I have accumulated is the joy of my life. If you, the actor, begin to encourage your curiosity about everything, you will find great pleasure in what you discover.

INFORMATION

In order to become conscious you must develop a hunger for information, reading, listening, watching and absorbing knowledge from a plethora of places—newspapers, television, movies, news programs, documentaries—and from people whose knowledge you respect. Personally I have a reading disability. It isn't dyslexia. I was just never taught to read properly. I read very slowly, one word at a time instead of taking the whole line in at once. Because of this disability I learned to compensate by listening. All the way through school and college I listened to the teachers and lectures and absorbed everything through the auditory sense. In addition I learned by watching films, television and so on.

I had an experience I think would be interesting at this point: Many years ago I was in a restaurant with my ex-wife. As we were having lunch, she mentioned a book she had read and began talking about it. I interrupted her, telling her that the information in that book had come from another writer and that this writer was expanding on the original thesis. She nodded, happy to get the information. She also mentioned an article she had read in a magazine. After she had shared its content with me, I told her that the information was incorrect and that the writer had gotten it from many other places. After two or three more of the same kind of responses, she slammed her fork down on the table, looked at me and asked, "Where do you get all this from? I know that you don't read much and..." At that point she stopped, looked at me for a long moment and said, "You son of a bitch, you watch movies!" Yes, she had gotten it. I watch thirty to forty movies a month. It is one of my great pleasures. And by watching all those movies I learn and absorb all of the research that all of those screenwriters have done to authenticate the content of the films they write! Those screenwriters possibly spend years researching their material, and I ingest and absorb it in the space of a two-hour movie. I also get a lot of knowledge from conversations I overhear while eating lunch at a restaurant. I feel that my brain is like a sponge and hungry for knowledge. In order to elevate your consciousness, you must create a great hunger to be informed.

COMMITMENT

To address those components of consciousness you must commit to being involved in each of the areas above. Find ways to become interested on the journey. Make it exciting, a game you involve yourself in.

Make the process a daily involvement. To discover and learn about subpersonalities you must be aware and conscious. When I started working with Hal Stone, the process he was using was *voice dialogue,* and at that time he said that subpersonalities and the way he was using the technique were a psychological tool. Later on in the work, he changed the emphasis and said that subpersonalities and voice dialogue had become a process for elevating consciousness. Commitment to elevating your consciousness is an ongoing process. If you follow all of my suggestions and you stay committed to doing the work, you will experience success.

CHAPTER 2

WHAT ARE
SUBPERSONALITIES?

ORIGINS AND ARCHETYPES

Even though I have already written about the archetypes in my last book, *A Second Chance at Life,* I feel that it is a necessary lead into this book, so I am going to borrow some of what I wrote. Subpersonalities originated in the work of Carl G. Jung, a Swiss psychologist and contemporary of Sigmund Freud. They were both eminent doctors of the mind but had very different concepts about the unconscious. Jung dedicated his entire life to pursuing the knowledge and mechanism of how the unconscious functions in our lives. Freud on the other hand thought that the unconscious was a gigantic dumping ground for our experiences, and while he did spend time exploring it, he never plunged to the depths that Jung went to.

Jung's concept of the archetypes is where subpersonalities originated. My exploration of those origins and Jung's conclusions led me to delve into two of his books, *The Archetypes and the Collective Unconscious* and *Man and His Symbols.* Here are a few excerpts from those books that describe the archetypes:

"While the personal unconscious is made up essentially of contents which have at one time been conscious but which have disappeared from consciousness through having been forgotten or repressed, the contents of the collective unconscious have never been in consciousness…but owe their existence exclusively to heredity…. The content of the collective unconscious is made up essentially of *archetypes*…definite forms in the psyche which seem to be present always and everywhere."

"In addition to our immediate consciousness which is of a totally personal nature…(even if we tack the personal unconscious as an appendix), there exists a second psychic system of a collective, universal, and impersonal nature which is identical in all individuals. …It consists of pre-existent forms, the archetypes, which can only become conscious secondarily and which give definite form to certain psychic contents."

"There is a good reason for supposing that the archetypes are the unconscious images of the instincts themselves, in other words they are *patterns of instinctive behavior.*"

"There are as many archetypes as there are typical situations in life…. When a situation occurs which corresponds to a given archetype, that archetype becomes activated and a compulsiveness appears, which like an instinctual drive, gains its way against all reason and will."

When archetypes are activated, "explosive and dangerous forces hidden in the archetype come into action."

"The main proof of the existence of archetypes is dreams, which are spontaneous, involuntary products of the unconscious."

"Elements often occur in a dream that are not individual and cannot be derived from the dreamer's personal experience. These elements are...mental forms whose presence cannot be explained by anything in the individual's own life and seem to be aboriginal, innate, and inherited shapes of the human mind."

"The term 'archetype' is often misunderstood as meaning certain definite mythological images or motifs. But these are nothing more than conscious representations...."

"The archetype is a tendency to form such representations of a motif.... There are for instance, many representations of the motif of the hostile brethren, but the motif itself remains the same."

The archetypes "are indeed an instinctive *trend* as marked as the impulse of birds to build nests."

There are two sentences in the excerpts above that I want to emphasize: "The content of the collective unconscious is made up essentially of archetypes... definite forms in the psyche which seem to be present always and everywhere," and "The main proof of the existence of archetypes is dreams, which are spontaneous involuntary products of the unconscious."

Here is a personal quote that I feel racks focus on the specific concepts of subpersonality exploration: "There are times," said Somerset Maugham, "when I look over the various parts of my character with perplexity, I recognize that I am made up of several persons and that the person that at the moment has the upper hand will inevitably give place to another."

I included all that because it makes an important statement about the origin of subpersonalities and the fact that the archetypes at the base of what are called subpersonalities are very well rooted in the unconscious. So when the statement is made that a person embodying a subpart is actually in an altered state of consciousness, it resonates with reality. Many psychologists and other practitioners have been working with subpersonalities for decades. A large number of books and articles have been written to explore in detail how subpersonalities can be approached, and there is a plethora of information as well as specific details on the Internet about how to use and explore the many techniques involved. In *The People inside Us,* one of the many books on the subject, John Rowan, a British psychologist, clearly suggests that subpersonalities are real entities that are part of who we are and that have an incredible influence on our lives and behavior.

WHAT IS PERSONALITY?

We often hear one person say about another, "He's got a great personality." So what does that mean? Is that the sum total of who that person is, that one description "a great personality"? The fact is that when people say that about another person, they are only relating to a small facet of that person's total personality. Infinite facets of behavioral qualities and emotional differences are contained in one's personality. One person may describe another as being humorous, open, charming and magnetic, while another describes that same individual as always angry and antisocial. So which one is right? They both are in essence. Whatever the stimulus, the reason a person behaves in a particular way is dependent on many things. The affable, charming person is responding to his environment or to the person or people present. He might have had a great day or he feels accepted and comfortable every time he is in the company of people who bring out all of his magnetic qualities and behavior. That same individual can be very off-putting and be behaving in a completely opposite way as a result of a different stimulus he is being affected by. So let's call those different personality behaviors *subpersonalities* at this moment for want of a better way to describe them.

BEHAVIORAL EXAMPLES OF PERSONALITIES

She is always complaining about something, always blaming somebody or something for her unhappiness. He never takes anything seriously, always joking, making light of some of the most serious events. He's a control freak! It's his way or the highway. She is constantly nurturing and taking care of whomever she is with. I think that all he thinks about is sex; he can't keep his hands to himself; women complain that he is too touchy feely, and they don't want to be around him. She spends a lot of time being really sad. It's difficult to be around him; it's like you have to walk on eggshells so as not to piss him off; he's always ready to fight; he seems capable of being violent. She seems never to have grown up—Alice in Wonderland; she spends a lot of time in her fantasy life. He is so judgmental you would think that he is a Catholic priest; he constantly criticizes everyone's morality; I have never experienced anyone so critical and mostly critical of himself. She is never satisfied; anything that she thinks is less than perfect gets her very angry. He is constantly pushing himself to do more, accomplish more; he never seems to be satisfied. He does nothing; always wants to kick back and bake in the sun. He is always being the activist, saving the world from one form of autocracy or another.

Those are just a few examples of what people say about each other, but there are so many more. It becomes a serious problem if those people get trapped in those personality behaviors, which quite often happens if the person is not conscious of what is going on. Many people live in a socially pleasing personality. Famous people promote loving and caring behavior for the world to see, but when they are not in the spotlight other parts of who they are surface.

Many years ago I was acting in a Twentieth Century Fox movie titled *A Private's Affair*. Gary Crosby played one of the characters. We became friends and spent a good deal of time between scenes talking about many things. I told him I had met his father when I was in the army. An artist friend of mine was doing Bing Crosby's portrait for the Pebble Beach golfing establishment, and I had visited the artist during the sitting. I had met Bing, who was very nice and affable and had included me in the experience. In a conversation with Gary I related that event, and he went ballistic! He ranted for many minutes about what a son of a bitch his father was, how selfish and abusive he was to all of his sons, emotionally and physically abusive. Gary hated Bing with such passion it was unsettling to me. One of Bing's other sons committed suicide, and the other twin I believe died at a very young age. So there is an example of a person (Bing Crosby) who to the world was an "American sweetheart" but in reality had a very powerful dark side. His other self was a subpersonality that would take over and wreak havoc on his family. This phenomenon is very common and very dangerous if there is no *aware ego* present. (I will explain that term later.) If a person moves from one subpersonality to another without being conscious of the changes, the situation can become very precarious; even more so, if someone gets trapped in a subpart or a triumvirate of "other selves," that can be tragic.

THE SUBPERSONALITY ARCHETYPES

The PROTECTOR, the PUSHER, the CRITIC (inner and outer), the GOOD FATHER and the BAD FATHER, the GOOD MOTHER and the BAD MOTHER, the PLEASER, the

WISE PERSON or the wisdom voice, APHRODITE—the female sexual energy—DON JUAN—the male sexual energy or subpersonality—the child archetypes (and there are many of them: the VULNERABLE CHILD, the FRIGHTENED CHILD, the LONELY CHILD, the MAGICAL CHILD, the REBELLIOUS SON/DAUGHTER, the MISCHIEVOUS CHILD, the OBEDIENT SON/DAUGHTER) the JUDGE the MESSIAH, the GURU, the MASTER CONTROLLER, the HERO, the KILLER, the WARRIOR, the SATANIC or DEMONIC energies, the SPIRITUAL or MYSTICAL energies, the ACTIVIST—those are some of the most common subpersonality archetypes, and there are more. By identifying them by name we become more aware of who they are and how they function.

An example of moving from one subpersonality to another is the fictional account of Doctor Jekyll and Mr. Hyde. In that novel Doctor Jekyll drinks some chemical concoction that he created, and in a short moment or two the good doctor turns into this evil person committed to evil acts and hurting people. The technique used to move from one behavior (subpersonality) to another is the chemical concoction. Is it a metaphor on the evil of alcohol, of drinking? It is certainly an example of how one subpart can move into an opposite other self. In terms of our work, there are numerous approaches for accessing the various subpersonalities. I will describe them all in detail in the next chapter.

THE THEORY: WHO ARE THE SELVES? HOW WERE THEY CREATED? HOW DO THEY FUNCTION?

At birth and at the very moment we become conscious the process begins. Our *primary selves* or subparts are created to protect the *vulnerable child* from harm and the consequences of life. They are the *subpersonalities* or *selves* which in the very beginning appeal to our parents or caretakers and receive approval. As we grow older and our sphere of relationships expands, we become aware of what behavior is acceptable and which is not. Thus the creation of the primary selves continues on into adolescence and often beyond —such energies as the PROTECTOR, the part of us that runs interference and protects us from harm and from doing the wrong thing, and the CONTROLLER, the part that calls the shots and comes into action to take control of our behavior when it feels there is danger or negative consequences. Those two often work together, as we move into one and then the other. A number of other selves are part of the primary-selves' category: The PLEASER is a subpart whose entire energy is devoted to doing the right thing and pleasing everyone. We have all experienced people who always seem to be concerned with pleasing and getting acceptance and approval. Another interesting subpart is the PUSHER, the one who is always there to push us to do things, to work, to achieve. This is the one who gets in our ear and whispers, "Get out of bed" in the morning and "Get to work," and who constantly reminds us that there is a lot to be done.

Next comes the INNER CRITIC, a part of us that is always criticizing us, that tells us that our performance isn't good enough or that we need to do more to accomplish our goals. It often teams up with the pusher, who pushes us to achieve while the critic stands in the wings denigrating our efforts. The inner critic is a very powerful subpersonality and very necessary to our life, as all of our selves are! But if it seizes control, gets into the driver's seat, and refuses to relinquish its hold, our life can become a living torment!

Another part, the MIND or intellect, is the one who thinks and evaluates things. Its emphasis is on intelligence; it puts a premium on knowledge and the use of the brain to accomplish our goals. In addition, the ACHIEVER is totally involved with accomplishment. If it takes over, a person can become blind with ambition and allow no room for anything else. Finally, the WORKAHOLIC dedicates its owner to working constantly, thrives on working, and sees little else in life except work!

As I said earlier, the primary selves are created to gain acceptance and approval, so some of them exist only in certain people, since which one gets formed depends on the environment a child grows up in and on the influence of the people in his life. If, for example, someone is part of a very religious or pious family, he will most likely develop a MORALIST subpart, better known as the MARTIN LUTHER subpersonality. Other selves can make up the primary-selves cluster, such as the PERFECTIONIST or the CONCILIATOR; however, those I have listed are the most common.

For every primary self you identify and become familiar with, there is an equal and opposite energy or subpart. So one of the opposites of the controlling part listed above might be the easygoing, permissive part that goes the way the wind blows. You have experienced people in that energy. They are kind of kickback and very allowing and accepting of everything that goes on around them. It is almost as if the entire sixties generation was infected by that virus. They were all inhabited by that subpart! The pusher's opposite is the beach bum, the part that likes to do nothing but vegetate and loaf. The opposite energy to the responsible self is, of course, the irresponsible self, while the opposite of the pleaser is the part that is self-involved and doesn't care what anyone thinks about him. It is a fairly antisocial energy. Those opposite energies are pushed into the background by the primary selves, because they pose a threat to the security of the individual. In some cases they even threaten the vulnerable child and some of the other child archetypes. If an opposite self is too threatening and even considered dangerous by the primary selves, it becomes a DISOWNED SELF and is *pushed way back into the unconscious.* The more threatening it is to the primary selves, the deeper it goes into the unconscious. Disowned selves have a need to be heard and recognized, however, and if that isn't done, they can become malevolent and dangerous. The deeper a disowned self is consigned to the unconscious, the harder it is to access consciously. If it is left there for too long, it will retaliate through the unconscious by creating issues, problems, and self-sabotage.

The disowned subpersonalities come to us in our dreams. They reach out for recognition and speak to us while we sleep, asking to be heard—which is another very important reason for us to pay attention to our dreams. Some of the selves are less dangerous than others, so they are more accessible through voice dialogue and other techniques.

Examples of opposites and disowned selves are some of the child archetypes—such as the magical child, the mischievous child (its counterpart, the obedient child, can exist as one of the primary selves), the vulnerable child, and the frightened child—as well as the warrior, the killer, Aphrodite or Don Juan, the satanic or demonic energies, the dictator, the beach bum, and a variety of others. Once you have identified the primary-self structure, you can pretty much expect that you will find its opposites in the disowned regions. Voice dialogue and some of the other techniques help you to communicate with the various selves and to liberate them, to create an aware ego, expand your consciousness and become cognizant of the forces that affect your life. Once you have established an awareness of those selves and their dynamics, they can no longer take control of your life. The aware ego sits between them and can hold them in balance, asking any one of them to relinquish its position and give way to another. It can raise or lower the energy of any of the selves and objectively relate to and include all of them.

The actor must become familiar with his instrument and with the mechanics of subpersonality work, and he should identify the primary-self and disowned-self structures. He must understand the dynamics of how they function as well as the "dances" they get into with other people. He can achieve this by doing voice dialogue or working with some of the other techniques involved, such as paying attention to his dreams or keeping a dream journal and identifying the voices of his disowned selves as they plead for attention and recognition. Immediately upon awakening, before one loses the dream, one should ask questions about who were the ones in it, what they were doing and what they said to anyone. One might even try some *active imagination* with the figures in the dream, as I will explain later. That is an excellent way of identifying disowned selves and learning about them and what they want.

There are times after having had a specific dream when, as a result of working with it, I receive a clearer picture of the message in it. I am able to identify with greater clarity a disowned subpart, whereas in the dream it was unclear to me who that was and what it was trying to communicate.

Becoming aware of the subpersonalities that inhabit us is a large part of the work we must do. Earlier I spoke of the importance of achieving consciousness and how essential it is to the discovery of the many subpersonalities that we encounter on our journey. The primary selves and the disowned selves are active in our daily life and behavior. If a person experiences an identifiable emotional response to an event or experience he or she is having and is unaware that his or her behavior is nothing more than the response to the stimulus that caused it in the first place, then the tendency is to repeat the emotional expurgation each time he or she is affected by a similar stimulus. He or she becomes a victim of his or her own behavior and has no control over it. It is important to understand that when someone is affected by an event, another person or other components of an experience and he becomes aware that his response and the ensuing behavior has elicited a subpart, he is then able to control the situation by involving an *aware ego* so that he does not become victimized by not being able to understand what is happening or how to defuse it.

In my introduction I said I was going to demystify subpersonalities, and that is what I intend to do. As we discover and give names to the various subparts, we are identifying facets of our overall personality. When we do voice dialogue, for example, we are exploring the network of our many selves, so to speak. By doing that, we begin to understand how and why we respond in a similar way each time we are confronted with a specific stimulus. Not only do we have the knowledge and power to understand why we are hurt by the impact of a harsh criticism from someone we respect and love, for example, but we also know which subpersonality is affected and responding to the criticism. Let us say that it is the vulnerable child or the vulnerable adult that is experiencing the pain and rejection. Because we have become aware of our personality facets, we can allow that self to receive the entire impact of the experience, knowing that there is something we can do about it. I am not saying that we should do something so we can avoid the pain involved; I am saying that now we have the awareness that what happened between us and the person who criticized us accessed a specific subpart of our personality, and as long as we do not get trapped in that subpart we accept the experience and allow for another self to move into the forefront position.

So many people live their entire lives in total ignorance about their behavior—why they behave the way they do, why they are so unhappy with their life and are continually confused about the way they feel. How many times have we heard people say, I wasn't dealt a good hand when I was born; luck is something I never had; I just don't know why I can't ever get it together; nothing I try ever works; I have never had a good relationship with a woman (or man); I guess I have never been in the right place at the right time? Yes, I do believe that luck does play a part in our lives and certainly in the success we achieve. However, it is not totally responsible for the direction our life takes. We are the responsible ones. We call the shots, and the success we achieve is dependent on how conscious we become. All of the examples I stated above come out of people trapped in a *victim* subpersonality, and they will stay there forever if they do not become aware of where and why they are trapped in that energy and what they can do about it.

I want all the readers of this book to approach subpersonalities without a sense that there is something supernatural or complex about the approach. All of the techniques, exercises and approaches of my system are practical and pragmatic tools to achieve organic results. And so is the megapproach subpersonalities.

In an earlier section I included a part on the origins of the archetypes, which made me assume that when an archetype is activated it creates an alternate state of consciousness. That statement is echoed in several of Hal and Sidra Stone's books. I myself have said it when doing acting workshops on subpersonalities, and I have mentioned the phrase in some of my other books. What it actually means is that when a choice, an exercise or a subpersonality access technique piques and elicits a totally unconscious response, the unconscious elevates itself into the conscious state of the person, which is when it's referred to as an altered state of consciousness. I wrote a book entitled *Acting from the Ultimate Consciousness*, where I describe ultimate consciousness as a place where the unconscious takes over and the actor does not need to do anything but get out of its way. That state leads to a level of acting that all of us devoutly wish would happen more of the time. One could describe it too as an alternate state of consciousness or reality. It would be a mistake for an actor to think or believe that every time he accesses a subpart he is in an *altered state of consciousness,* however. If that is an expectation, and when it doesn't happen the actor feels that he failed, the tendency is for him to try to make it happen and when that fails to fake it. The reality is that you do not need to achieve an altered state of consciousness in order to successfully inhabit a subpart. It is somewhat similar when an actor in a scene crosses that line into what I call the ultimate-consciousness experience. Whatever the trigger was that piqued the unconscious and brought it into the conscious sphere, that phenomenon can occur the same way when accessing subpersonalities. It is usually connected to a very impacting experience. Both of those states of consciousness happen when the actor works for something that dislodges that unconscious memory bank.

THE ELEVENTH LEVEL OF CONSCIOUSNESS

Many years ago I came up with what I called the *eleventh level of consciousness*. It is one of my concepts and is not at all scientific. It does, however, relate to a real phenomenon. I chose the number eleven since I felt that an actor must be totally involved on the first ten levels of consciousness in order to be able to organically experience the behavior in a scene and on the eleventh level be aware of what he is doing.

I can't say how many times I have been asked the same question by actors: If you are experiencing a total reality on the stage, how is it that you don't really kill the actress at the end of the second act? The answer is that *there is a part of you that knows that you are acting.* That part of you lives on the *eleventh level* of your consciousness. Why the eleventh level and not the seventh? Because I felt that if you could be involved on the first ten levels of consciousness in the reality of the play, that was a deep enough involvement not to be interfered with by the eleventh. Of course, the number eleven is just an arbitrary choice of mine.

I had been working with the craft for some time when I began to relate to this concept. Sometimes as an actor I would get involved more deeply than other times. When the level of consciousness was too close to a third or fourth level, I was aware of being on the stage, of acting, commenting on my work and falling short of an involved organic experience. With more work and increased proficiency with the craft, I found that my acting consciousness level drew farther and farther back in terms of my awareness of being on the stage. However, at the same time, this eleventh level carried me to the places on the stage where I needed to be; it remembered my lines and cues and served me well without interfering with my involvement in the reality of the play.

It is like having a dream. You are asleep and dreaming. You are totally involved in this dream, but there exists a part in you that knows that you are dreaming. It is called lucid dreaming and does not occur every time you dream. The eleventh level of consciousness is something like that, only not quite so remote.

How do you create an eleventh level of consciousness? Well, not by pushing a button, that's for sure! It is a phenomenon that evolves with the work. The more you know how to apply the process, the greater the involvement in the realities produced by that process. In other words, the more you believe in the here-and-now reality, the farther back you push your consciousness that you are acting. So, as you evolve into a craftsman, a by-product of your growth is the eleventh level of consciousness.

Sometimes people ask, What if one doesn't have or develop that level of consciousness? To that I say that person has no business being on the stage. He is dangerous and shouldn't be involved with acting!

When the unconscious takes you over onstage, the results are usually electrifying. It is that experience that we look forward to each time we act. The eleventh level of consciousness does not interrupt or interfere with that connection to the unconscious; it just seems to take three steps back.

Next time you step onto a stage, take an inventory of your consciousness level and become aware of how it moves around as you become more involved and affected.

I included the definition of the eleventh level of consciousness so that when an actor accesses a subpart, he or she needn't feel that it is not enough to be inhabited by the energy of another self without experiencing an altered state of consciousness. The foundation of all of my work is not to act at all, but to become a "professional experiencer," which means to really experience what the author says that the character is experiencing. When a person (an actor) elicits a subpersonality, the goal is the same—to experience that subpart totally.

EXPERIENCE HUNTING— CHOICE HUNTING

Quite often I ask my students to do a choice hunt after they have finished doing the preliminary preparations of relaxation (eliminating tension from the body and mind), sensitizing (elevating the accessibility of each of the five senses one at a time), and then doing personal inventory. We do a choice hunt at the beginning of class about twice a month. I encourage all my actors to do choice hunts on their own about two or three times a week. It is a very meaningful involvement, and as a preparation it affects the actor on multiple planes. First, it elevates his emotional level and quite often heightens his vulnerability, which makes him more capable of addressing the emotional requirements of a scene or monologue. Secondly, it allows him to explore and discover a multitude of new choices that he can use in his work. The third and maybe the most important element in choice hunting is that it can, and often does, create a conduit into the unconscious, which when activated brings exciting unconscious life to his work.

For the purpose of addressing subpersonalities I have chosen the words *experience hunting*. It is essentially the same process, but it emphasizes the search for the multifarious subpersonalities that exist or for when and why they entered into our life. What happened and when did it occur so as to make it necessary for that other self to come into our life? Having an understanding about the way the primary and disowned selves function is somewhat of a prerequisite to experience hunting. However, you can be doing voice dialogue or other techniques simultaneously.

THE VARIOUS APPROACHES USED TO EXPERIENCE/CHOICE HUNT

There are a number of exercises to do this. They can be done aloud or as inner monologues.

I'M FIVE YEARS OLD AND I...

The exercise should start with an early age; for example:

I'm five years old, and I am in kindergarten and I like playing with clay. I am five years old, and my teacher Miss Shaunesy yells all the time. It scares me. We have milk in the morning. I like chocolate milk, and I like Laura; she's pretty. My older sister takes me to school every day. I tell all the other kids that she is my mommy. My real mother is old, and my sister is young and pretty like all the other mommies. I'm five years old, and I like playing in my backyard. I like playing with my next-door neighbor, Earl, but he's moving away. His family is moving to another state. I'm really sad about that. I cried last night. All my brothers and sisters are much older than me, and sometimes I feel very alone. They all have things to do and places to go. I'm five years old, and I had the measles. I scratched everywhere! I'm five years old, and I want to be a grownup. I'm five years old, and I'm afraid of the dark. I sleep with a light on. I'm five years old, and what if I die? All of my brothers and sisters talk to each other, but they don't talk to me much. They hug me. I talk to myself a lot, and sometimes I imagine that I am someone else living with a different family that likes to play with me.

Whatever you might get from this exercise, it is obvious that this child is coming from a *lonely-child subpart*. This can go on until you run out of things that you remember from that time. And of course you can start at a later age, but hopefully it will be a young age. Many people have difficulty remembering things about their life at very early ages. You go from five to six to seven to eight and so on. While you are in the process, many events and experiences come up where you are able to see when certain energies entered your life. Those subpersonalities usually are the result of traumatic and impacting experiences. Their entrance is usually a way of protecting yourself from threats to your safety or wellbeing. Protection is most often in the forefront when a subpersonality comes into your life when there is some kind of threat or trauma, such as your parents divorcing or a death in the family. Disappointments, rejections and abrupt changes in environments can also elicit other selves.

MEANINGFUL EVENTS AND EXPERIENCES

Another way to experience-hunt is to remember specific times in your life when a memorable thing happened—graduation from high school or college, receiving awards, winning a race in a sporting event, the first time you fell in love or had sex, the death of a parent, getting your first job, obtaining a promotion, and so on. Bring those memories forward and then try to remember what was happening in your life just around that time, before and after those events. By doing that, you will remember so many more things that happened, and by exploring those events you will understand how and when certain energies (subparts) inhabited you.

MOVIES, SONGS, MUSICAL BANDS AND GROUPS

We all remember a film or musical play that was a favorite at a very different time in our life. We also remember the Beatles, the Monkeys or Elvis Presley. If you go back to those times and to all the memories of that period, many more experiences will materialize for you. Once you discover something that you have not remembered or thought about for many years, you can explore those events and discover many of your personality changes. Learning about the plethora of subpersonalities that inhabit us leads to a much greater understanding of who we are and how we function. Going back into your life opens many doors that have been closed for a long time. Remembering your experiences stretches your memory and enables you to get a more complete picture of your evolution through your life. It is a wonderful way for you as an actor to discover choices that you can employ in your acting; and if you emphasize becoming aware of the various subpersonalities that existed and the others that appeared later, you will have a greater understanding of the component parts of your personality.

CHAPTER 3

THE APPROACH TECHNIQUES FOR ACCESSING SUBPERSONALITIES

There are a number of approaches that I have used in my subpersonality workshops. Having so many of them enables the actor to select the ones that fit the specific dramatic situation and are the most technically capable of addressing the time and space issues of the scene involved. For example, let's imagine that the actor is moving from one emotional state to another and needs to quickly access a subpart to accommodate the behavioral change. He cannot access any given subpart that takes a lot of time to reach. So he might just *roleplay himself into the desired other self.*

Here is a list of approaches:

Voice dialogue, using a journal, using a tape recorder, using movement and dance, using art—

drawing and sculpting—using choices, music, role-playing, externals, and imaging.

All of those approach techniques work. Becoming familiar with them is what the actor must do. Once he is facile with each of them, he has a cornucopia of tools to bring forth any number of subpersonalities.

VOICE DIALOGUE

Voice dialogue is a two-person process. The facilitator talks to the various selves of the person being facilitated as they manifest themselves, or he can ask to speak to a particular one. The technique allows the person being facilitated to disengage those selves from her total personality or, in other words, to relate to them as separate parts. The facilitator addresses each subpersonality as a distinct entity, encouraging it to talk and express itself. At certain intervals in the process, he might ask the subject to move into her aware ego, at which time she separates herself from the part that was responding and physically moves to another place in the room. When the subject feels detached from the self that was just there and experiences objectivity, the facilitator can comment to the aware-ego state on what the self said and where it was coming from. The subject being facilitated thus becomes conscious of her subparts, while at the same time creating a facility to control them. Each of the subpersonalities has a distinct energy pattern that inhabits the being of the subject physically, emotionally, and in all behavioral ways. Being in one of the selves transforms the person and seems to put her into an altered state. In my own personal experience with voice dialogue I have witnessed incredible changes while the subject was in a particular personality. Often, her physical appearance was altered. Her facial structure, as well as her physical posture and attitude, seemed to change. It is truly a remarkable phenomenon. Each of our subpersonalities experiences and looks at life very differently, and each has its own responsibility to our life. Going from an aggressive protector-controller to a vulnerable child, for example, can usually transform the person being facilitated from a tall, imposing physical being into a visually smaller, frailer person with a higher, halting voice. It happens right before your eyes and is an amazing experience.

THE VOICE-DIALOGUE PROCESS

The facilitator must relax and stay in a relaxed state, become objective, and in no way be threatening to the subject being facilitated. He should acquire a benevolent demeanor, in which case the subject will be more willing to come to the forefront. He must never disagree or engage in conflict with the part that he is relating to. It is quite common for the facilitator to want to succeed in the facilitation, so he must become aware of his own pusher or critic and avoid getting derailed by his own subjectivity or any other energies that might obligate him to encourage a successful session. He must be able to hear the vocal changes, however subtle they are, see the physical cues and notice the emergence of different energy patterns while conducting the voice dialogue.

The facilitator starts the session by encouraging the subject to speak about anything, particularly what is going on in her life at that moment. By starting that way he will be able to identify who is there, what sub-part or self is speaking, and what other voices might come in, which might interrupt that part. The facilitator must become aware of the alterations in the voice and the physical changes that happen, no matter how subtle they are. He can get an overview of the person right at the beginning. The ability of a facilitator is subject to how sensitive and how perceptive a person he is. Facilitating is a learned ability which grows with repetition and practice.

A number of years ago, in 1983, I shared a weekend workshop with Hal Stone in Houston, Texas. He took the first day and I the second. After introducing the group, whom neither of us knew, he had them doing voice dialogue in the first half-hour of the day. I asked him if there could be damage from any inexperienced facilitator, and without hesitation he assured me that it would not happen, that the primary selves would not allow the subject being facilitated to go anywhere the protector-controller thought to be dangerous. He was right. It was a very successful day. Everyone facilitated and was facilitated. On the second day I taught the acting part of the weekend, utilizing what the participants had learned about each other and bringing that knowledge and experience into the scene parallel I had asked them to do.

Example of Voice-Dialogue Facilitation

The facilitator is usually seated facing the subject, who should start in a standing position but may sit at any time during the facilitation. The facilitator might be silent for a few minutes to allow the subject the time to get comfortable. Either one may start to speak. Usually it is the facilitator:

FACILITATOR. Hi, how are you?

SUBJECT. *(After a short pause.)* I'm all right…I guess.

FACILITATOR. What do you mean you guess? Are you unsure of how you are feeling?

SUBJECT. No, I'm not unsure, but I'm a little nervous about talking about myself…I mean that I don't really know you, so I'm not sure about what you want to hear.

FACILITATOR. *(Being aware and making notes that the subject is sensitive and somewhat insecure and that she obviously wants to please him.)* Well, why don't you just talk about anything you want to?

(At this point the facilitator begins to notice a change in the subject's demeanor: she stands much straighter, her posture becomes rigid, and her voice drops several octaves.)

SUBJECT. What do you want? What are you asking for? Do you want her to bare her soul to you? *(All the subparts refer to the subject as separate from themselves. It is "her," not "me.")*

FACILITATOR. *(Immediately noting the energy shift.)* No, I don't want you to do anything that isn't comfortable! Who are you? I mean, I am interested in knowing you. I can see that you are very reluctant to expose the way you feel. Are you protecting her?

SUBJECT. What I do is take care of her, because she can't do that for herself. She is too weak to stand up for herself. I jump in to see that she stays out of trouble and doesn't get into any uncomfortable situations.

FACILITATOR. Oh, I get it! Well, that is a very responsible job, isn't it?

SUBJECT. I feel that it is nobody's business what I do for her. And I feel that you are invading my space. The reason that I run interference for her is that she's not very strong, and sometimes I think that she's not very bright either.

(At this early stage in the facilitation, the facilitator takes a brief inventory of what subpersonalities he has detected from the attitudes and behavior of the subject. At the beginning, the subject, Marie, was in one of her child energies, possibly her shy child. Her pleaser was also subtly present. Soon after, the *protector/controller* jumped in and took over. In addition there seemed to be a very active critic—which would indicate that those three are working together. At this point the facilitator might decide to continue to speak to the protector.)

FACILITATOR. I see...so in essence you take care of her?

PROTECTOR. Yeah, that's right! She has got into a lot of trouble before.

FACILITATOR. Trouble? What sort of trouble?

PROTECTOR. Well, when she was a little girl and before I was able to help her, her parents would verbally abuse her.

FACILITATOR. You mean that they would yell at her and criticize her?

PROTECTOR. That's putting it mildly! They yelled constantly and called her stupid and even began telling her that she was retarded.

FACILITATOR. That sounds very serious! Is that about the time you came into Marie's life?

PROTECTOR. No, I was always there, but there were others that kept me from expressing myself and coming to rescue her. I tried—God knows that I tried!

FACILITATOR. Who were the others?

PROTECTOR. Well, you see, Marie always wanted to be loved by her parents, and so she was very obedient and would do anything to please them.

(Making a mental note, the facilitator understands that Marie had a very strong pleaser as a child and also a well-nourished obedient daughter. They were obviously strong enough to make it difficult for the protector to do her job adequately.)

FACILITATOR. How were you finally able to succeed in being heard?

PROTECTOR. Well, I am not sure. It seems that I got some help from somewhere, but I couldn't tell you where it came from. It was about the time Marie went into the first grade that she started to be belligerent and disobedient. She became downright rebellious towards everyone and everything. It was at that time that I could express myself, and I'm telling you that things really changed.

FACILITATOR. There must have been some kind of internal change for Marie at that point. Well, it was very nice talking to you, and possibly we might continue this later, but I would like to speak with Marie now. Would you mind? *(When the facilitator asks to speak with Marie, he really means her aware ego.)*

PROTECTOR. Yeah, that's OK.

(At this point the subject moves away from the protector/controller energy to another place in the room.)

(The aware ego is not a subpersonality. It is a state apart from the energies and other selves of the subject. The creation of an aware ego is very important to be able to identify the various subpersonalities as they manifest in a person. It is an aware and objective state of being that can identify a person's other selves and is able to move whichever subpart is there out of a control position and to ask another to move into the forefront. The aware ego is created the first time a person is facilitated. Because of the facilitation, the subpersonality being facilitated is recognized and no longer exists in the shadows.)

FACILITATOR. Hi, Marie! Are you in an aware-ego state?

AWARE EGO. Yes, I'm here.

(Visually Marie's entire behavioral state has changed. She seems much more relaxed and together.)

FACILITATOR. I assume you heard everything that went on and was said?

AWARE EGO. Yes, I did. It's very clear what's going on. I noticed that the protector was quite belligerent towards you in the beginning but seemed to mellow out as you talked to her.

FACILITATOR. Yes, I noticed that too. Were you aware that there are a few energies in operation there? I mean that there is quite a bit of critical energy as well as some responsible judgment taking place.

AWARE EGO. A number of them are looking out for her. I'm aware of them, and it gets clearer all the time—I mean, about how they operate.

FACILITATOR. Have you been able to sit between those selves? Have you been able to talk to them?

AWARE EGO. Well, not a lot yet. I kind of just came into being.

FACILITATOR. What do you mean by that?

AWARE EGO. It's only recently that Marie started to become conscious of all of those selves. With the help of voice dialogue and a few sessions *I was created.*

FACILITATOR. I see. Well, now that you are here, you can relate to the various parts of Marie and ask them to back off or lower their energy.

AWARE EGO. Yes, I intend to become much more involved, and I feel stronger and more aware each time we do voice dialogue.

FACILITATOR. Thank you. It is a pleasure to know that you are here and ready to balance all of Marie's energies. Could I speak to the first one who started in this session?

AWARE EGO. Sure!

(She moves from her place in the room and wanders for a few moments until she settles on a place further back. The facilitator, sensing that this self is reticent and tentative, waits a few moments before beginning to speak.)

FACILITATOR. Hi, how are you?

SHY CHILD. *(Moves a foot or two backwards.)* I'm all right. How are *you?*

FACILITATOR. Oh, thank you for asking…I'm fine …anxious to talk to you.

SHY CHILD. Why? I mean, why do you want to talk to me?

FACILITATOR. Well, in the few moments that we had earlier I felt a very nice, warm quality from you, and I wanted to get to know you better.

SHY CHILD. You like me, huh?

FACILITATOR. *(Hearing a little pleaser energy.)* Yes, I do like you. Is that important to you?

SHY CHILD. Well, yes! I mean…I was never sure that her parents liked me. I would look into their eyes, and I never saw anything that said they liked me.

FACILITATOR. Did you do anything about that? Did you talk to them about whether or not they liked you?

SHY CHILD. No, I was afraid to ask them that. I was afraid that they would say no.

FACILITATOR. So what did you do?

SHY CHILD. I was quiet…I was very good…I did things that I thought they would like.

(At this point the facilitator notices that there are a couple of voices coming through. The physical change in the subject is incredible. When she was in her aware ego, she seemed mature, self-confident, and relaxed. When she moved into the shy-child energy, she seemed a foot shorter and slightly bent forward, and her voice became thin and a little inaudible.)

FACILITATOR. I hear someone else trying to break in here. Would you please move over a little and let me talk to her? I promise I will come back and talk to you later.

(The shy child is a little reluctant to give up the space but with hesitation moves a couple of feet to her right.)

PLEASER. Hello! She's so shy, but really nice, don't you think so?

FACILITATOR. Yes, I do. She seems very nice.

PLEASER. I try to help her do the right thing. She's very fearful you know!

FACILITATOR. Yes, I can see that. Tell me about *you*. What do *you* do?

PLEASER. Oh, well, I make sure that everything goes right, that everyone is happy. I try to make sure that everybody likes her. It isn't always easy to do. *She* comes out and wrecks everything! I don't know what to do about her!

FACILITATOR. Who is *she?*

PLEASER. The one nobody can do anything with. She's so spoiled she's a brat!

FACILITATOR. I'm sure that's very difficult to handle, especially if she won't listen to anyone. I'm curious about her. May I speak with her for a moment or two?

PLEASER. Oh, I'm not sure that you want to. You see, once she gets out she never wants to leave! Well, all right, I'll help you.

(She moves out of that space and walks to within two feet of the facilitator, in an in-your-face position, so to speak. Again the subject's entire persona has transformed: she is standing with her weight shifted to one side, hands on hips, with an incredibly challenging attitude.)

FACILITATOR. Hi, it's nice to meet you.

REBELLIOUS CHILD. Don't give me that crap! You don't care anything about me, and I don't know who the hell you are and I don't care!

FACILITATOR. I see. Well, as a matter of fact I do care, and I would like to hear more about you.

REBELLIOUS CHILD. Like what do you want to hear? I'm not going to do any of that goody-goody crap for you! I'm sick of all the crap that goes on around her. If it weren't for me, they would have rolled over her a long time ago—you know, her parents, the kids in school, everybody!

FACILITATOR. I see that you are very concerned about her well-being. It seems that you have also protected her quite a bit.

REBELLIOUS CHILD. I don't know if you can call it protection. I just stood there and wouldn't do anything I didn't want to, and none of them could make me either!

FACILITATOR. Well, I think that you are very determined, and that's good! You seem very mature also.

REBELLIOUS CHILD. I had to grow up real fast around here! If I couldn't handle it, who would? I mean, those others wanted to protect her, hide her, but I wasn't about to let them put her into some kind of box—know what I mean?

FACILITATOR. Yes, I think I do. I really enjoyed talking to you. I learned a lot about her life, thank you. May I speak with Marie now?

REBELLIOUS CHILD. Yeah, I guess that's OK, as long as you didn't ask to talk to any of the others. *(She moves back to where the aware ego was sitting.)*

FACILITATOR. *(Taking a moment to make sure that Marie's aware ego is back.)* Well, hello again! So you can get a clear idea of all of those selves, right?

AWARE EGO. Yes, I'm getting clearer about them. I still don't know who they all are or how they function, but I'm learning very rapidly.

The facilitator does a brief recap of everything he observed. He might ask Marie to come and stand at his side in the WITTNESS STATE. The witness state is a nonverbal self who is not attached to the outcome of the session or the dynamics of the relationship between the selves. It *witnesses* what happens, takes it in, but is not involved in communicating with any of the subparts. It is different from the aware ego in that the latter is totally involved with the communication of the selves and can control their energy and participation. As he recaps the entire session, the facilitator makes some comments and shares his conclusions. At this point he will return the subject to one of the primary selves, because those are the parts that are most familiar to her, the ones she grew up with and is most identified with.

FACILITATOR. *(Speaking to the aware ego.)* Thank you, I'm sure that each time you experience a session you become more aware of everything.

(The aware ego gets up and moves to another place in the room.)

This example was a capsulized version of what a voice-dialogue session is, and it was designed to give the reader an idea of the process. An average session can last as long as an hour or more, as the facilitator spends more time with each of the selves. In this instance, the emphasis was *instrumental*. The purpose of the session was to help the subject develop an aware ego and become knowledgeable about the energies that exist in her. For an actor this is a very important prerequisite. She must first understand who her subparts are and how they function before she can expect to use this process as a choice approach and acting tool. Once she's familiar with how to access the various subpersonalities, she can use voice dialogue to elicit the desired ones to do her acting, but she must initially understand who they are, where they are, and how to call them forth. Using this as an acting tool takes two experienced people, the facilitator and the subject. They must both know what they are doing and have experience with the process.

An addendum to that example of voice-dialogue facilitation is to emphasize the purposes of the process. We start to explore the various techniques for accessing the multitude of subpersonalities that inhabit a person because they are very important tools for raising our awareness of the energies that are there and of the selves that enter into our life as we evolve. Most people are totally unaware that mood swings and unpredictable behaviors are normal phenomena. They live an entire lifetime and never become aware or conscious of the dynamics of the energies that come into them, and as a result they are helpless to understand and do anything about them. So many of the psychological problems that plague them are never understood or dealt with. So a major reason for doing voice dialogue is to become conscious of the presence of those other selves that inhabit us.

Another reason for starting with voice dialogue is that it is the first time that we learn how to create an aware ego. Without the creation of an aware ego a person is unable to deal with or control the various subparts. It is not enough to be aware of the other selves that are there or come in later; you must be able to move them in and out of a control position. That is the job of the aware ego! It is the facilitator's responsibility to get the person being facilitated to separate from a subpart, step back and become aware that the aware ego is not part of a subpart. The creation of the aware ego in the beginning is a very important responsibility of every facilitator.

Since this book is for actors, another purpose for voice dialogue is to identify other selves that the actor can access to use in creating the experiential life of the character he is obligated to create. It is a wonderful journey into the discoveries of a myriad of incredible choices that he can use in his work.

This is one that I have never written about before and it came to me while I was looking at my view of the city and musing. Let us suppose that a director directing a play or film understood what each character in the piece was impelled by—meaning a specific energy the character was inhabited by—and that he could identify all of the characters in the piece and the behavioral "dances" that went on between them; couldn't he do voice dialogue with all the actors involved, creating an ensemble of all the subpersonalities and how they affected each other? Besides using all the skills he needs to conduct the piece, a director can include his facilitations as a directing technique that would probably deepen the involvement and relationships of all the actors in the piece.

USING A JOURNAL

This is another way an actor can use to access subpersonalities. This approach has advantages: first, because some subparts are reluctant to communicate verbally, so using the silence of writing in journal form allows them to respond; and also because it affords the actor privacy to work with subpersonalities when he finds himself in a situation where he needs it.

The actor can use a legal pad or any kind of paper that can retain numerous entries. He must promote being in an aware-ego state before he begins. He starts by writing: "I would like to speak with...." Almost any of the subparts that he would like to engage with, for example the vulnerable child. He must leave enough space on the pad for the subpart to respond, hoping in this instance that it does respond. Sometimes a subpart will need to be asked more than once in order to speak.

VULNERABLE CHILD. *(Hesitantly.)* I'm not sure what to say or what you want from me *(pause)*. I'm afraid to be here.

I. Well, I promise that you are safe with me in this place, and you don't have to respond if you really do not want to. I will wait until you feel you can.

VULNERABLE CHILD. I always get hurt. No matter what anyone says or promises I always get hurt! People are selfish and insensitive and they don't care if they hurt you.

I. I understand how you feel, and please take your time and express everything you feel. I want you to trust me and I'm OK with not talking for a while if that helps you to get comfortable with me asking questions.

VULNERABLE CHILD. Well, I wish that I wasn't so afraid all the time. I would like to be free, play and enjoy myself. There are so many things that I would like to do, but I'm sad a lot of the time! So many things make me sad and unhappy.

I. Well, would you like to share the things that make you sad and unhappy?

VULNERABLE CHILD. No, what good would it do? Would it change anything? I don't trust you!

(At this point in the facilitation another voice comes in with an aggressive attitude. The facilitator (I) recognizes that it is the protector that has jumped into the process. The facilitator must make an adjustment immediately.)

I. Hello, I understand that you don't want me to hurt him, so let me try to assure you that I only want to allow him to be heard and express his feelings.

PROTECTOR. So what's your motive? Is this a game you like playing?

I. I assure you that I mean no harm. Obviously, you are there to protect him and I appreciate that.

PROTECTOR. OK, I will let you talk to him, but be careful and be patient with him.

(At this juncture the facilitator (I) waits for a few moments, and then he addresses the vulnerable child again.)

I. Hi again, how do you feel?

VULNERABLE CHILD. *(Mumbles inaudibly.)* I guess I'm alright doing this. You seem nice and you are not pushing or pulling at me.

I. Well, I want you to know that it is nice being with you.

I know this seems a little strange and somewhat "woogie," and I said that I would take the mysticism out of the exploration and usage of subpersonalities. I will therefore explain this so that it becomes a practical tool that an actor can use. It is a self-facilitation. Starting in an objective place, an aware-ego place, the actor (facilitator, I) starts talking to, and asking questions of, a particular subpart that he wants to access, allowing that energy to inhabit him. He goes back and

56

forth between the facilitator and the subpart that he has accessed.

I know it sounds weird, but I have had success using this technique. It takes practice and a willingness to inhabit the various subparts being called forth. If the actor is using the technique to practice using a journal to access subpersonalities, it is a good training involvement. If, however, he is using it to prepare to access a particular sub to address the obligation of a scene he is about to do, then it is a tool, an approach to inhabiting an energy, another self, to address the responsibility of a character in a scene.

USING A TAPE RECORDER

This is somewhat similar to journalizing, except that it is verbal. Out loud the facilitator records his questions first and leaves blank space on the tape for the subpart to respond. Then the actor moves into a subpersonality (the one that he wants to access) and records the responses. In a sense it is somewhat like roleplaying himself into the desired subpart. (I will explain roleplaying later.) It becomes a dialogue which goes back and forth between the facilitator and the self being facilitated.

It is important that the self being facilitated move into another space, a few feet away from the facilitation. This is also true for journalizing. Each self is an energetic entity and occupies a specific space. When moving from one subpart to another, the subject must physically shift positions. This process takes time to accomplish and must be practiced again and again for the actor to become facile with shifting from one place to another. Literally inhabiting the energy of another self takes imagination and a willingness to let it come into you.

USING MOVEMENT AND/OR DANCE

There are lots or reasons why there are so many techniques for accessing subpersonalities. Many sub-parts are only affectable by certain stimuli, and quite often are only sensitive to approaches that are not verbal. Those energies are more instinctual than rational. Their makeup is nonverbal and they respond on a physical level rather than with words. Some of them exist in the sensual or sexual areas or at the primal levels of our being. Sometimes they are part of the child archetypes—the mute child subparts. You can access them by experimenting with a wide variety of movements and dances, while discovering who they are and what appeals to them and elicits their energy. It can go from an aggressive primitive abandonment to very delicate graceful movements and gestures.

For many years I have been using an exercise in my classes that I call *primitive abandonment*. It is an instrumental approach to getting the actor down into a more aggressive primal energy as a tool for accessing deeper emotional states if he is unable to otherwise reach those places. It has been an incredible approach technique in the area of promoting instrumental freedom impressively and expressively! However, it also has the ability to access basic animal energies and can often call forth the *warrior* and *killer* subpersonalities. Quite often, moving in delicate circles, sawing the air with the arms flailing can also appeal to the actor's other selves. Practicing with a plethora of movements and dances is a way to explore and discover who is there and wants to be seen and felt.

At one of my weekend workshops that I call jamborees I was demonstrating the use of a samurai sword I have as an object that comes into contact with the body, another of the choice approaches that are part of my system. In the demonstration I became a Japanese ninja warrior replete with the physical, emotional and vocal attributes of the characters in the film *Seven Samurai*. It accessed a subpart that had all the attributes of a historic ninja warrior. Shadowboxing, throwing punches into an imaginary opponent can also access certain aggressive energies that manifest themselves as definitive characters that can be used to address dramatic material.

USING ART—DRAWING AND SCULPTING

This is yet another approach technique for plumbing the depths of all of the incubated subparts that exist within us. I do not believe that anyone has given a number to how many archetypes and subpersonalities actually exist. Maybe we are capable of having within us an infinite number of other selves. Their makeup is very often complex, and it is entirely possible that we will never access or know them all. Have you ever wondered why some people end up doing what they do in their lives? What is it that creates a technical genius, someone who has a penchant or a talent that seems to come from nowhere, an inborn ability to comprehend complex theories and mechanical concepts? Where does a computer genius or a musician who at an early age can master numerous instruments come from—a Mozart, a Van Gogh, or the unending numbers of gifted people who seem to have been born with their unique and unusual abilities? Have those people lived before and have they been reincarnated? We could ask those questions indefinitely without ever finding the answers. There are many theories: that those talents are due to genetics—are in the DNA or are inherited—or they are the result of their environment, of exposure to certain influences from others and so on. But perhaps they are also the manifestation of a subpersonality that has embedded itself in the person's life and does exactly what it does. Maybe that "artistic subpersonality" took hold of Van Gogh's life and never let go. If you know something of his life, you would know that he was so obsessed with painting that he spent the money his brother Theo sent him on oils rather than food. That reality in itself verifies that his obsession was a subpersonality in control of his life, and without an *aware ego* he spent the rest of his life servicing that obsessive subpart!

There are several ways you can approach the area of drawing or painting. Get something you can draw on, a sketch pad for example, and color pencils, crayons, charcoal, water colors, oil paints or any other medium. With a blank page in front of you encourage yourself to start drawing whatever comes up and is translated through your hands. In a stream-of-consciousness manner, encourage anything you draw to be there. Allow whatever feelings are stimulated by the pictures to affect you. Be aware of the energies produced by what you have drawn that are running through you. You may not be able to put into words what you think those energies are in terms of sub-parts, but you are definitely being affected by drawing. It is evident as a result of what you are experiencing that drawing does appeal to a part of you that stimulates specific states of being.

Another interesting exercise is to draw the previous night's dreams. Shortly after awakening, draw your impressions of each of your dreams, using your feelings to guide your hand. Encourage whatever ends up on the pad to be there, no matter how abstract it might look. Don't concern yourself at that point with interpreting the drawings or understanding their relationship to your dreams. Just allow yourself to feel whatever they stimulate. Be aware of the specific energies that come to the surface, and if possible, identify your responses in subpersonality terms.

Sculpting is very much the same as drawing or painting, with one very important difference: the physical process! When sculpting, we use our hands to make contact with the clay or whatever other material we might use. In some way this direct contact seems to appeal to other parts of our subpersonality structure. For some reason that I cannot explain, that contact and the molding process itself seem to stimulate other energies. In preschool, in kindergarten, children finger paint and use clay and other molding substances. In other words, we all begin to create with our hands at a very early age; but in most cases we lose this connection as we grow up and matriculate into the higher grades. It is possible that those early childhood experiences are somehow linked to subpersonalities that did continue to evolve and were consigned to the unconscious—only to be resurrected by the process of sculpting. Of course, that is just a theory!

The process of sculpting is similar to drawing. The actor sits with a clump of clay, takes a moment or two and then starts by kneading the clay and molding it in a stream-of-consciousness fashion. He continues until he creates something. That something might be anything, a person, an automobile or anything else, whatever it may be. He should be aware of any feelings or impulses that come up while he is sculpting. It is quite possible that his involvement with the clay will pique some subpersonality with whom he is not familiar and possibly create a conduit into the unconscious, and that the process will continue to access other energies coming from that childhood unconscious memory bank.

Many years ago at a five-day workshop that I took with Hal and Sidra at their ranch in Northern California, our group sat at a table outdoors on an incredibly beautiful day, sculpting with clay. Some of us created human figures, while others made pottery. Some attempted to sculpt the figures that had appeared in their recent dreams. It was an amazing experience; everyone, including myself, was affected in such an impacting way that it actually changed our physical appearance. We sat looking at each other without saying a word. After some minutes we began to discuss our experience, and everyone agreed that there was a different energy dynamic between us, and that many of the people were behaving quite differently.

USING CHOICES

Among the processes that access subparts, this is one of my personal favorites. I really like this approach because there are no limits to the number or kinds of choices that you select. So what is a choice, or what do I mean when I say choice? A choice is not a decision. A choice can be a person, a place, an object of any kind, a weather condition, a sound, music, clothing, the taste of food, the sound of a telephone ringing, a train whistle in the distance—in other words a choice can be anything that has an effect on you. Even though I have used all of the techniques to access the various subpersonalities that I was working with, I favor this one because it has a built-in fail-safe device. Let me explain that: When an actor uses a choice to appeal to a particular subpart, his involvement with that choice keeps him focused on it and on his response to it. In other approaches there is sometimes the possibility for him to impose behavior or fall into representing his involvement in the process instead of being involved on a level where his concentration is selfless. Perhaps I am partial to this technique because it is one that I myself created specifically for actors.

Earlier in this book I talked about how important it is to elevate your awareness and to become conscious on the highest level possible. It is important that you discover on a daily basis how things affect you and whether the people, environments, events and experiences stimulate certain energies and access your other selves. Make note of those changes in your feelings, and even if you are not preparing to act, catalogue all of your discoveries for future use. Become increasingly conscious of how the various objects that you come into contact with work to access the different energies. As you become more aware of which choices appeal to your subpersonalities, you will be able to use the right ones when you are trying to access a specific self.

Some selections are just a matter of common sense. Let us suppose, for example, that you wanted to access and liberate your sexual subpart. The choice would obviously be something or someone that stimulates sexual attraction or lust or both, such as someone that you have those feelings for or maybe just a sexual fantasy that you create. If you wanted to access the child archetype, you would choose an object or experience that you know would appeal to the specific child energy. It could be a toy, a stuffed animal that you slept with as a youngster, a playground that you enjoyed, friends who were in your life at that time, or even a favorite television program that was important in your childhood. Let us say that you wanted to access your warrior or your killer energy. Again, you would select an object or person that piqued it. I mentioned earlier how a samurai sword affected me. In the same way, when I pick up one of my rifles—even when it isn't loaded—and I walk around with it, I feel aggressive and after a short while very much in touch with my warrior. With a minor adjustment, while still holding the rifle, I can elicit the killer part of me. All I have to do is imagine all the people in the world I would like to kill—people like the dictators who have been responsible for the deaths of thousands of people, or serial killers, particularly the ones who hurt little children. I might use any of the choice approaches to create those choices. For my rifle example it was available stimulus; the people could be created through sense memory or by using imaginary monologues or evocative images. A very rich choice approach that is multifaceted in accessing subpersonalities is objects that come into contact with the body. The rifle example fits into that category. Many objects, clothing, and jewelry, when we are either wearing or holding them, appeal to our various selves. In short, there is a bottomless well of choices that stagger the imagination. Explore them and use them to access your subpersonalities and communicate with them. So much of who we are as adults is the result of our meaningful experiences in our early, formative years. I had a lot of difficulty while growing up. I was teased, abused physically as well as mentally. I grew up in an ethnically mixed neighborhood and my family was one of only two Jewish families that lived there. As a result I suffered the kind of bullying that one only reads about. I developed an ability to run like lightning so I could get home before those who were chasing me could catch me. As a result of the incredible damage I suffered, I created a plethora of choices that accessed a whole legion of subpersonalities. Almost all of the child archetypes were involved, as well as the warrior, hero and killer subs. My fantasies were filled with Superman retaliations against the guys who abused me, and to this day all of those choices work to access the subparts that I call forth.

USING MUSIC

Music can definitely fall into the choice category, but the reason I'm separating it is that it is so vast in kinds, styles and sounds. It is so rich and so varied that it could be used somewhat exclusively by itself. It appeals to many parts of us. Listening to different kinds of music can stimulate patriotism, overwhelming passion for our country, sexual and romantic feelings, or anger; it can elevate our vulnerability and take us down memory lane. Its impact on us is phenomenal. Of course, using music as a choice will almost always have an effect on us, but not necessarily access a subpart. So it is dependent on us as actors to be aware of when a piece of music appeals to another self and connects us with that energy. When I do a subpersonality jamboree, I ask all the actors to bring in three separate and varied pieces of music. I want them to experience the impact of each piece to delineate the different feelings and impulses that they stimulate.

Think about all the movies we have seen in our lives and how the score of certain films creates the mood and the emotions of the characters in the piece. When we think of some of our favorite films, we hear the music that was in the background. Take for instance the movie *Jaws*. That music is unforgettable, and the memory sends shivers down your spine! So many films were supported by a great score that we have difficulty separating the music from our emotional relationship to the film. I have used music as a choice in many of the parts I have played, in theater and film. In talking to many of the actors I have worked with over the years, I found out they too have depended on music as a stimulus to address emotional obligations for the part they were playing. It is a great bonus when the music that an actor selects also accesses a subpart that carries him through the scenes that he is doing. Since I have been involved with subpersonalities for so many years, I have become very familiar with the multifarious subs that function in my life, and it is easy for me to identify a particular subpart I wish to elicit. With so many years of experience with the process I am never at a loss for why I am feeling or behaving in a specific way. I identify who is there, and if I'm not happy with that one in the driver's seat, I call upon my aware ego to move it out of a control position.

Start experimenting with various types of music to see what appeals to your subpersonalities. I have a very strong hero subpart, for example, and when I hear patriotic marches, such as any of the pieces that John Philip Sousa wrote, I am immediately inhabited by my HERO subpersonality. As an actor using the process, you can work with the music as available stimulus as a preparation to access the subpart that you are attempting to access, or if you are in the scene and need to create a particular piece of music, you would have to work to create it sensorially.

ROLEPLAYING

Roleplaying is something I devised as a technique for accessing the other selves. It is a one-person involvement and similar to voice dialogue insomuch as it is a facilitation done by the subject. You might refer to it as *voice monologue!* It is an approach technique that is initiated by the actor starting from an aware-ego state. This particular approach is quite dependent on the actor's experience with subpersonalities, since it is entirely dependent on knowing where a certain energy is and how to access it. The actor asks for a specific subpart to come forth and speak. Again, this technique should only be implemented after the actor has had considerable experience with voice dialogue and is quite familiar with the existence of the energies that inhabit him. If the actor attempts to access his various selves before knowing who they are and what degree of difficulty he will experience in getting them to cooperate, he will most likely fail to elicit and access them organically. What that means is that he will resort to imposing his concept of that subpart rather than actually inhabiting the energy organically. All of that being said, it is one of my favorite techniques for accessing those other selves, and it can be done quickly and easily.

After achieving an aware-ego state, the actor simply asks to speak with a specific self. The major difference between this and voice dialogue is that this is not a two-way conversation. Once he has elicited the energy of a subpart, the actor encourages it to express itself. At this point, when the subpart begins to speak and the actor is fully inhabited by the energy of who-ever is there, he must not attempt to talk to it, since it will be confusing to that subpart. This is a really good technique, because the actor can request a specific sub-part to come forth in order to address the obligation of the material he might be working on. As I said earlier, roleplaying is for the more experienced actor who has developed a relationship with his many selves. When experimenting with the approach, he may just ask whoever is there to come out and speak. In that case the subpart that is accessed might in a stream-of-consciousness fashion just begin talking about what-ever is on the mind of the actor at that moment.

Example of a Stream-of-consciousness Monologue

OK, so what am I doing here and what do you want? I'm a little tired and I really do not want to speak, at least not about anything that is deep. It isn't that I am lazy; I just don't feel like dealing with any-thing heavy, get it?

In order to move out of that stream-of-consciousness monologue, the actor must go to the aware ego to ask for another voice (or self) to come into the picture. This is very important! I spoke earlier of the eleventh level of consciousness. Without that fa-cility the actor would not be able to employ the aware ego. That makes a very important statement about sub-personalities as a choice approach. In the original pre-cepts of working with subpersonalities, I maintained that when a person is inhabited by a subpart he can be in an altered state of consciousness, and if that is true there isn't any way he can go from one subpersonality to another! There are times when being inhabited by another self goes deep enough for the actor to experience an altered state of consciousness, but he must still have an eleventh level of consciousness available to him.

I know that this seems a little complex, but in my attempt to demystify subpersonalities as a viable approach, I must include the eleventh level of consciousness in order to justify the ability to go from one subpart to the next without imposing that ability, since that would only cause the actor to short-circuit the reality!

USING ROLEPLAYING TO ADDRESS THE OBLIGATIONS OF DRAMATIC MATERIAL

Once an actor identifies the obligation that he wants to address in a particular scene, he can decide which of the approach techniques to use in order to access the right subpart. He should always select the least complicated approach. If he does select roleplaying, then from an aware-ego state he should ask the subpart that carries the emotional life of the character in the scene to come forth. If that self is experiencing the emotional life required by the character in the scene, the actor will fulfill the scene experientially.

EXAMPLES OF CHARACTERS IN PLAYS AND FILMS THAT CAN BE APPROACHED BY ROLEPLAYING

In the play *The Lady's Not for Burning* the leading character has an expurgatory tirade criticizing one of the other characters in the play. This would be a perfect selection to access the inner-outer critic subpart.

Addressing the other character:

"You bubble-mouthing, fog-blathering,
Chin-chuntering, chap-flapping, liturgical,
Turgidical base old man! What about my murders?"

The character speaking those lines must be filled with enormous critical energy.

The character at the opening of the play or film *Glengarry Glen Ross* is filled with criticism and judgement of the group that he is speaking to.

In both those examples the actor must roleplay himself into the inner-outer critic and also be able to access and include the judge in the second example.

Accessing the Inner-Outer Critic

Before doing the scene the actor relaxes, clears any mental background noise and gets into an aware-ego state.

ACTOR. I would like the part of me that is critical to come out. I want you to talk about all the things that you are critical about that are happening in my life and all the other things that go on in the world that you find reason to be critical of.

(After a brief pause the actor should move into a different place in the room or on the stage until he finds where that critical energy is.)

INNER-OUTER CRITIC. I'm so sick of my hesitation to tell people what I think! I swallow so much shit trying to be a good guy. There are so many bullshit people that I have to deal with, lazy shits that want the world to do their work for them. Actors are among the laziest people on the earth, and they expect me to take up the slack for them. Everybody wants a free ride! I spend money every time I walk down the street—those fucking street people with their hands out! Get a job, you lazy fuck! You look healthy enough to work. This fucking city, the traffic is unreal at any time of the day; doesn't anybody have a job? Who's driving at noon congesting the streets and the freeways?

That tirade can go on for as long as he has things to be critical about. Once the energy is in place and the critic is actively expressing himself, the actor can do the scene. If he uses the tirade as a preparation, he can be audible, but if he needs to access the critical energy while doing the scene, he can do that tirade as an inner monologue.

Roleplaying is a wonderful approach for accessing subparts, and the more you work with it the quicker you will become facile with it.

EXTERNALS

Externals is one of the thirty-one choice approaches that are part of my system. It is one of the five megapproaches, and I am including it as one of the techniques used to access subpersonalities. It is a powerful choice approach and can be used in many venues to address the fulfillment of dramatic material. There are four parts to it: getting a sense of animals, of people, of inanimate objects and of insects. In my second book, *Irreverent Acting,* there are specific technique approach charts that teach you how to study animals and people and how to work to get a sense of them through your own body. I am including this approach because quite often it has the ability, once the actor inhabits the animal or gets a sense of another person, to elicit a usable subpersonality.

The technique is used to address a wide variety of material obligations. It can create character behavior as no other choice can. It piques emotional life that is sometimes primordial, and it stimulates a thought process that few other choice approaches can produce. It is a dynamic approach and can be used to access subparts in the primal areas that are stimulated by getting a sense of an animal and translating that energy into a human carryover. By retaining it and using it to appeal to the primitive areas of who we are, we can access the earth energies and instinctual subparts. In my personal experience working with externals, I was able to elicit many of the other selves that I personally have used as an actor. I have already mentioned that the *primitive abandonment* exercise also accesses the subparts that are responsive to those energies. Many of the exercises and techniques that I mention in my books often dovetail into each other, so it would be a very good idea to look at the externals section in *Irreverent*

Acting. Besides animals and people, the other two parts, inanimate objects and insects, provide incredible experiences once you get into exploring them.

As is true with all five megapproaches, externals could constitute a complete approach process to acting all by itself. Exploring it is like walking into another universe.

DEFINING MEGAPPROACHES

I am inserting the definition of megapproaches here because I have mentioned them several times. I have thirty-one choice approaches in my system, five of which are megapproaches. As I mentioned earlier, a megapproach is a choice approach so rich, dense, and complete that if the actor wanted to, he could use it to create an entire acting technique. Since there are so many tools related to the craft, however, why just settle on one?

The five megapproaches are:
Sense Memory
Affective Memory
Externals
Subpersonalities
Imaging

ANIMALS

When I first began to look into using animals as choices to address characters in plays or films, I had no specific technique for observing them and learning how to use them. At Northwestern University my teacher had just told us to go out and study animals.

When I was in Martin Landau's class, he too had suggested that I study animals, but he had given me a little more information to go on: "Study their rhythm and limitations," he had said. At least that was a start, and from there, in the space of a whole year of visiting the zoo three times a week, I created a complete process for observing and studying the component parts of each animal in order to be able to practically apply the techniques and use them to address characterization. I would go to the zoo, observe a particular part of the animal, work on it, go home and practice getting a sense of that part; I would go back to the zoo the next day and add another part to become facile with. For a little more than a year I worked exclusively with the gibbon, which is part of the ape family. Once I could successfully get a total physical sense of it, I was able, using the techniques that I had created, to work with other animals at the zoo. I found that I could get a sense of every animal I had decided to explore!

That all happened long before I got involved with subpersonalities. Whenever I was able to achieve a complete sense of any animal, I knew it! It is an undeniable feeling! It completely takes you and your body into another dimension. You feel the animal inhabiting you. Everything changes; your rhythms change, physical mannerisms that are not you appear, and you move, talk, relate and behave differently. I found that it transformed me and that I was able to address the character in a unique experiential way. It was sometime later, after being exposed to the subpersonality process, that I realized that I had actually been experiencing other selves inhabiting my work as an actor. I am aware that if you, the reader, really want to be able to use animals as part of the externals choice approach, you must accept that it's going to take a lot of work. The result of that work commitment is incredible and well worth the effort!

For decades I had been using externals in my scene work in class and professionally in films. I would approach a character, thinking that it would help me to define his behavior if I explored the use of an animal. In so many instances the results were mind-boggling! Translating the animal energies and carrying them over into human behavior added so many facets to the character physically, emotionally, intellectually and psychologically! At that point in my journey I had not been introduced to subpersonalities, so I just accepted the wonderful results I received from the process. However, in retrospect, I was actually accessing other selves without really knowing it at the time.

My involvement with externals seriously started in my acting class with Martin Landau. I was doing a scene from *Desire under the Elms*. My character, Eben, was a young man, a farmer with very little education or worldly experience. He had a very rural level of consciousness and was very territorial about the ownership of his farm. I'm sure that he only bathed every couple of weeks, had dirt caked under his fingernails and cow dung on his boots. Abby, his father's wife, was attempting to sexually seduce him in order to eventually take ownership of the farm. I worked on the scene diligently and did it each week in class. Each time Marty's critique was the same: "Eric, I just don't believe that you are an illiterate, uneducated, un-evolved farm boy!" This went on for twenty weeks, twenty probably being the number of times that I attempted to get into this character. Marty continued his critiques by telling me that I was a college-educated Jewish guy, who had grown up in a big city and that my reality was poles apart from this character's. I could have just accepted that and moved on to another scene closer to who I was. But, no! I was not going to abandon this scene or this character; it would have haunted me as an "incomplete" in my life.

I gave it a lot of thought and finally came to the conclusion that Eben was lower on the human evolutionary scale than I, and if it was so, he must also be closer to being an animal. So I decided to explore the ape family and to observe and work with a gorilla. Since I had already been experimenting with the gibbon, moving to a larger ape was an easy transition. I worked on the gorilla for several weeks, going back and forth to the zoo. I would bring the gorilla translation into my rehearsals with my scene partner, who at that time was one of the five actresses that I burned out with my obsessive repetition of the scene. When I finally did the scene in class, Marty jumped out of his chair yelling and pointing his finger at me: "Yes, yes, that's it! You got him, Eric. I believed you. It was transformational!" I shared my process with him and the class, very proud of my accomplishment. It was truly transformational. My entire body, mind, speech and movement embodied someone else. It was me, but it went beyond what one might consider acting. I was filled with an energy I had never experienced before.

In my present level of awareness and years of experience, I really believe that it was my first experience with subpersonalities.

Many years ago I was cast as a Middle European assassin in a Kraft two-part television show. The character's name was Tippo, and he was described by his cohort as someone who enters a room and leaves without being seen or heard. I used that description as a guide to choose an animal that had that kind of stealth of movement. I selected a leopard, went to the zoo and worked for three days on getting a sense of that animal before starting the film. Tippo was a cold-blooded killer on a mission to assassinate a high-ranking official at the UN. It was a great role, and it afforded me a lot of latitude creatively. When I think back to that time, I remember feeling things that went beyond just getting a sense of the leopard. My thoughts and desires were filled with what we now define as a killer energy. I was possessed with it throughout the filming. I received comments from the director and some of the other members of the cast that my behavior was truly frightening. At lunch break I noticed many of the actors would purposely walk a wide track around me. I considered that a great compliment.

After I got involved with subpersonalities and created the various approaches for accessing our other selves, I began using externals in my weekend workshops on subpersonalities. I asked the actors in attendance to explore animals, people and inanimate objects to see what subs were piqued by their creation. We had great success in using externals to elicit a large number of subparts; and so externals became one of the techniques we use to access the various subpersonalities that address characters in plays and films.

So if you are interested in how to develop the ability to use an animal to access a subpart, you must learn how to observe animals and explore working to get a sense of one. If you follow the steps, the *approach technique checklist* below will lead you to successfully acquiring the ability to inhabit the creature physically.

APPROACH TECHNIQUE CHECKLIST

Observe the animal for:

1. **Overall rhythm:** Watch the animal, observe its rhythm and practice its movements at home. Take this back to the zoo, and repeat often. Carry that rhythm into your whole body.

2. **Leading center:** Look for the part of the animal that would cross an imaginary line first. That would be its leading center. Practice the use of that center in relation to your own body. Repeat this process many times.

3. **Secondary center:** This is the part of the animal's body that closely follows the leading center. If you watch the animal carefully, you will see which part of its body seems closely attached to its leading center and follows it. It's important to successfully identify both leading and secondary centers and to be able to experience them through your own body.

4. **Limitations:** Become aware of the animal's specific limitations, and add them to your

involvement one at a time. For example, most animals cannot stand erect; apes do not have a prehensile thumb and need to grab objects with their whole hand. Practice at home; go back to the zoo to see how accurate you are.

5. **Centers of weight, balance, and power:** One at a time identify where the weight is centered and where the balance and power of the animal are located; for example, in big cats the power is in the hind legs, which propel them forward when they move. Usually, the weight centers are also the power center, but that is not a hard-and-fast rule. Separate the centers; then put them back together.

6. **Isolations:** Practice isolating the parts of your own body such as your head, your thorax, your abdomen and your extremities, so that you can move them independently of each other. Do the same with the animal.

7. **Corresponding and contrasting rhythms:** Identify the various rhythms and work with each one separately. Then put them together. Keep repeating the process until you can get your body to function in corresponding and contrasting rhythms like the animal you are working with. Take a chicken for example: its head moves in a contrasting rhythm to its feet.

8. **Species and individual mannerisms:** Do the same thing as you did in the previous section. Once you have defined a specific mannerism,

repeat working with it until it becomes a part of your sense of the animal.

9. **The sounds of the animal:** While observing the animal, become aware of the sounds it makes. Identify where they originate so you can repeat them.

After you have spent a lot of time following the approach technique checklist you will find that all the elements will come together to accomplish a complete sense of the animal.

WORKING WITH ANIMALS

Certain animals by their very nature appeal to certain subpersonalities: Because simians are closer in their structure to humans, actors are attracted to the APE FAMILY—gorillas, chimps, gibbons, orangutans—and it seems easier to work with them and translate the sense you achieve to human behavior. As I mentioned earlier, I personally spent a whole year observing and getting a sense of the gibbon, which allowed me to create the blueprint or chart that I eventually used when working with all the other animals. Many characters in plays and films are very apelike in their physical and emotional behaviors. In the play *The Hairy Ape,* written by Eugene O'Neill and later made into a film, the main character is very apelike in his behavior and relationships. William Bendix, who played the main role, I'm sure had no idea how to approach the role with externals or subpersonalities. He was a good actor but worked from an intuitive place. He also played a basic character in *Lifeboat,* where he was again successful fulfilling the character. I mentioned earlier that I used a gorilla in a scene from *Desire under the Elms.*

THE BIG CATS—lions, tigers, leopards, and mountain lions—are all meat eaters and predators. There is a plethora of other animals in the kingdom, such as squirrels, possums, raccoons, and in another category, monkeys and so on. Before deciding on a particular animal, you should explore many. When you find one that resonates with you and stimulates the life of the character that you are playing, you may use it to address the many character elements and hopefully elicit a viable subpart. Here again, I mentioned earlier that I used a leopard for the character Tippo in the Kraft Suspense Theater two-part television show that I did.

Other exciting categories to explore are birds and reptiles—snakes of all types, alligators, etc. There are so many species of birds and reptiles to choose from. I remember that an actor in one of my classes was in a film where he was playing a very stoic killer, who was very still, but deadly. In one of the scenes he lunged towards another character and sliced his throat. The movement was shockingly quick with no advance warning. The actor picked a Komodo dragon to use as a choice. He went to the zoo for a whole week and worked with the reptile. He said he was very success-ful fulfilling the character's behavior. In *End as a Man,* a play by Calder Willingham, to play the leading role, Jocko De Paris, a complete sociopath, I used an Amer-ican bald eagle as my choice. The reason I picked it was the static power and lethal potential I sensed from that bird just sitting on a tree branch. I felt that he possessed the power and ability to pounce on prey in a split second. That choice did access a part of me that was right for the character. In retrospect I feel that it elicited a combination of two subparts, the killer and the satanic energies. I was able to move back and forth between the two.

I mentioned that I went back and forth from home to the zoo and back home again. Actually, it isn't necessary for you to go to the zoo. You can watch videos on animals and their behavior. You can rewind sections and pin down certain movements and mannerisms. A number of channels feature documentaries that explore a large variety of animals: The Animal Planet, the Smithsonian, Nova, National Geographic, and so on. Many people live with animals—dogs, cats, rabbits, birds of all kinds. Since they are there all the time, you may observe and work with them on a daily basis. A number of actors who have worked with me actually had a menagerie in their house and backyards. I am thinking of Brook who has what could be considered an animal petting zoo in her yard. She even has a small pig. One time she brought a white rat to class, whose name eludes me at the moment.

THE CHRONOLOGY OF EXPLORING AND USING ANIMALS TO ACCESS SUBPERSONALITIES

To use animals to access subpersonalities:
1. At first familiarize yourself with the *approach technique checklist* when observing the animal

at the zoo or in other venues. Follow it scrupulously. It is a very specific blueprint for achieving success.

2. Explore a wide variety of animals, becoming familiar with the process and experiencing the effect physically and emotionally. At this juncture you are not to obligate yourself to elicit any subpersonality. You are just exploring and experimenting. It is important to isolate the parts of the animal in your own body. You must repeat each element suggested on the checklist. For example, working with the leading and secondary centers, repeat moving through them a number of times. Do the same with the rhythms and limitations. Go back and forth between observing the animal and working away from it. When you return to the animal, see what you retained and what you did not. Include the specific species mannerisms of each animal that you work with.

3. After a period of time, begin to encourage yourself to identify any energy that might be another self. It is *not* difficult to know how it feels when you are inhabited by a subpart. It has a very identifiable impact on you physically and emotionally. It affects your mental state and creates thoughts that can be surprising. At first, you may not know what subpersonality it is or if you can even name it.

4. After following the step-by-step process, you might start to identify the behavior of a charac-

ter in a play or film. Once you feel that you have a sense of what energy and subpersonality is impelling the character's behavior, look for an animal that you can explore with the goal of accessing the right subpart to address that character.

HOW TO IDENTIFY WHAT SUBPERSONALITY IS IMPELLING THE CHARACTER'S BEHAVIOR

When reading the script these are the things to pay attention to:

What does the author or screenwriter say about the character when describing him?

What does the character say about himself?

What do the other characters in the piece say about him?

What are his actions and behaviors throughout the piece?

Once you have explored all of those elements you should have a pretty good idea of what subpart or subparts are responsible for the way he relates to the other characters and for his overall behavior.

Having all this knowledge about the character will help you to find the right animal to explore. Certainly it will help you to identify the categories of animals that fall into a certain group.

TRANSLATING THE ANIMAL INTO HUMAN BEHAVIOR

This is a very specific process and must be done in order to translate the impact of the animal into being erect instead of being on all fours. The translation should be done in stages, slowly and at first retaining the energy fully. As you continue the translation, you can slowly make it more subtle, working in stages and hoping to retain the sense of the animal as you become more and more human. It is a very common experience to lose the connection while translating and have to reinvest by getting down on all fours and re-experiencing the animal as before. You might have to go back and forth several times in order to retain the animal in human terms.

It may seem like a lot of work to use this technique to access subpersonalities, but it is well worth it. There are easier ways to elicit subparts, but I have personally found that somehow the *externals* choice approach is very rich in its rewards. There is an added bonus involved in these techniques, and when you are successful in achieving a sense of an animal in translation, even if it does not access a subpersonality, it will transform your physical and emotional life in multifarious ways that fulfill many of the character's attributes and psychology.

PEOPLE

Working to get a sense of another person is much like working to accomplish a sense of an animal. The main difference is that there is no need to translate it from the animal attitude to human behavior. You follow the checklist in the same fashion as you did with the animal. There is no species element involved, since while there are many differences between people, we all are part of the same species. Some adjustments must be made; for example, limitations can be structural, acquired, or physiological. Mannerisms, tics, twitches and other personal issues can be incorporated. Weight, balance and power usually manifest themselves in the physical structure of the person you are working for. If the person is heavier than you, you must accommodate that sensorially. Accomplishing the leading and secondary centers, the rhythms, mannerisms, limitations and specific peculiarities of the person will lead you to be able to inhabit that person and in many instances will access an identifiable subpersonality.

I have always thought that the external behavior of a person is a mirror of what the person is like internally. If that internal reality is a self, you might be able to access it simply by getting an external sense of the person. So I explored people in an attempt to find out what their inner life was like. There were times when what I experienced was uncanny. I was really getting a sense of the person's inner life, complete with his personal points of view, his thoughts, attitudes and specific sense of life. I did this for quite some time, not only for acting purposes, but because it became a very rich and rewarding involvement. I would study various people, people I knew and people who were at a distance, and after a period of working with a particular person, I began to feel things—thoughts, reactions, and judgements—that were not me. It is like that old method-acting joke; one method actor talking to another: "If I was you, and I am…" I'm not saying that if you get a sense of another person you will always be fortunate enough to embody the inner person. You will, however, be able to find out if you can use your responses to access a specific subpersonality.

Besides working with people you know or study at a distance, you can work to get a sense of someone famous, such as a movie actor or a celebrity in a political area. Having watched actors on the screen for a better part of my life, I am able to pick out mannerisms or specific rhythms; and in just getting a sense of a few of those characteristics, I am able to inhabit the entire person. For example, John Wayne had a very individual walk, a kind of gait, and when I hook into that walk I am able to get a complete sense of him. I can do this with a number of actors. When observing a person, look for distinctive behaviorisms that you can grab onto. Work with those elements, which will help you to inhabit the whole person.

When I did subpersonality jamborees at my house in the mountains, we would go to the village and study people. The actors would each pick a person and unobtrusively follow him or her for as long as possible. They would look for the centers, limitations, rhythm and mannerisms, using the time to observe the person walking, sitting in a restaurant and talking to other people. When they returned to the house, they would attempt to get a sense of the person they had worked with in the village, discussing the components and exploring the subpersonality potentials.

INANIMATE OBJECTS

Nonliving things, inanimate objects of all kinds, are yet another part of the externals choice approach that can be explored to access subpersonalities; for example, an overstuffed chair, a lamp, a piano, a bottle, a standing ashtray, a bicycle, a picture hanging on the wall, anything at all. It must be a stationary object that is not in motion but is totally static. If you select an object that has movement, such as a metronome that is moving back and forth, you are crossing into another choice approach called *essences and abstracts*.

Achieving success with inanimate objects depends more on your imagination than on applying the standard approach to externals. There are no active rhythms, tempo or mannerisms to address, so you begin the exploration by assuming the physical position of the object that you have chosen to work with; you attempt to sensorially get a sense of its mass, weight and bulk, and then try to get a sense of its static rhythm through your own body. I know that this sounds bizarre and somewhat abstract, but I have personally had a great deal of success using this particular technique. Many of the actors that I have worked with have had breakthroughs using this approach. Once you feel inhabited by the static energy of the object, you slowly translate the physical feelings into active movement.

You must do this slowly and in stages so as not to lose the connection with the object. For example, let's say that you have chosen to work for a large overstuffed chair. After assuming the physical attitude, or position, of the chair and working sensorially to create its bulk and weight, you continue to explore the static rhythm and physical feelings throughout your body, sensorially feeling the fabric and detecting the odors that you create imaginatively. When you are totally impacted by the object, you slowly translate it into active movement. Retaining the energetic impact that you have experienced, you are ready to determine how it affects you. Are you aware of any energy, thoughts, and feelings that you have accessed as a part of yourself that can be described as another self? Certainly the translation into human behavior has had a meaningful effect on you, but is it a subpart? Your involvement with the chair may not have elicited a subpersonality; however, there is a multitude of inanimate objects that you can explore that might lead you to experience success.

INSECTS

If you approach this using the chart, you will find that it is difficult to observe insects in the same way as animals. They move too fast and are so small that it is hard to determine leading and secondary centers as well as rhythms and mannerisms. It is somewhat easier with larger insects. (Spiders are not categorized as insects because they don't have antennae and wings. They are called arachnids.)

I would not have included this area except for the fact that I have experienced success with it. A few of the actors I have worked with in the externals techniques have also had surprising results getting a sense of insects. Once, as we were working on externals at my house in the mountains, an actor named George got a sense of a praying mantis. The response he experienced was mind-boggling. He turned into that insect right before our eyes. He looked more like an insect than a human being. It completely transformed him! His behavior was frightening. When he returned to himself, there was a carryover from the experience that affected him and obviously accessed a very noticeable change in his persona. When I questioned him, his responses were guarded and somewhat defensive. There was a discernable change in his personality, which went beyond the usual experiences of the process. I am sure that he accessed a very strong subpart that occupied his entire being. What that other self was, I don't know and I believe he didn't either. The experience was incredible for everyone who was there. There were other instances when people would access meaningful responses by using an insect and translating it into human behavior.

IMAGING

Imaging is another one of the five megapproaches, and it is like opening a door into a completely new universe. I wrote a three-hundred-and-ninety-six-page book on the subject, entitled *Acting, Imaging and the Unconscious*. The uses of this approach technique are multifarious. It is a process to access and communicate with the unconscious, stimulate and interpret dreams, address and solve health issues and imaginatively to relate to and access subpersonalities—just to mention a few of the areas where it is actively and successfully used. In acting terms it is also used as a choice approach to address the obligations of dramatic material. It is largely dependent on sense memory, on using the five senses to create objects, people, places, and so on. Like many of my exercises and approach techniques, imaging is a complete process, and there are components involved in being able to successfully use it. For our purposes here I will explain how it is used as an approach technique to access and relate to subpersonalities.

I invented this approach at a weekend subpersonality jamboree at my house in the mountains. It is a highly imaginative technique. You must be willing to freely encourage your imagination to create and believe in what you have created.

After deciding on a specific subpart that you want to access, you visually create it across the room from you. Working sensorially, you create a complete visual manifestation of what the subpersonality looks like. It can have primitive and animal-like features and stature. It can be of a different gender, have an avian body, be a gargoyle, a child of a certain age, a reclusive figure without a face, and so on. There is no limitation to the kinds of images that you can create. Let your imagination fly! Be specific in creating the image of the subpart that you have selected. There are two sensory approach techniques you can use: you start by asking sensory questions related to the subpart that you are creating and responding with all five senses simultaneously. After you have successfully begun to get a response, you move into the second sensory technique which is called *imaging sensations,* which means that all five of your senses are still responding simultaneously, but you stop asking sensory questions. I know that it takes practice to acquire the ability to do that, since it is different from the original sense-memory technique. At first, all five senses are responding to the sensory questions, but as you go on with the exploration, you may discontinue the questions and just respond to the object you are creating with all five senses.

Example

Before you start the imaging process it is important that you get into an aware-ego state. You must not be attached to any of your subparts since they could directly interfere with your ability to create the subpersonality that you have selected. Relax and get comfortable, and decide which of your other selves you have decided to create. Let us imagine that you have decided to access the Martin Luther subpart, which is the moralist energy. To help you get started you should explore and express your own moralistic judgements (*our society has turned into a sewer—drugs and whores on every corner, a complete lack of spiritual connection and a complete disregard for other human beings*). You can then choose a place in the environment you are in, and start the process. Do not just pick any spot; take the time to feel where that energy might inhabit. Begin to imagine what he might look like. Do not impose a concept, but image it intuitively. Once you have a sense of the general outline or appearance of the subpersonality, you can begin to create it through imaging, using all five senses in either of the imaging techniques. You might want to start with sensory questions or just use *imaging sensations* throughout. If you start with a mental image or a visual concept, you can expect it to undergo some changes as you pursue the process. It is one thing to have a mental picture based on a concept, but what your senses produce is quite another image. Having decided to work with the Martin Luther subpersonality, you begin to image it in the place that you have selected:

How far away is he from where I am sitting? (All sensory questions are responded to with all five of your senses simultaneously. Remember that the senses do all of the work.) *How tall is he?... What is the color of his hair...shape of his face...nose...mouth?... What is the color of his eyes?... Do I hear any sounds?... What are they like?... What is the expression on his face?... What is the attitude of his body?... What is he doing?... When he speaks, what does his voice sound like?... What is the pitch?... What emotions is he expressing?... Can I tell how he feels by the sound of his voice?...* (At this point in the imaging process you might want to stop asking questions.) *I see him moving towards me....* (All of your senses are responding at one time.) *I hear him ranting against the sins of the world. His voice sounds deep and guttural. I can almost physically feel the impact of his rage. I can actually see the fire in his eyes. Anger exudes from every pore in his body.... I see him looking at everything in this place, his lips curled up in judgement.*

All of the imaging sensations take place in the senses, and the thoughts are a result of what you see, hear, feel, taste, and smell. There is no verbal or intellectual involvement.

After taking whatever time you need to create this subpart, when you feel that he is there in front of you and he dimensionally exists, get up and go towards your creation and walk into it, inviting all of it into your body, your being. Allow yourself to experience anything that happens while you inhabit your creation. It is almost like putting on an overcoat. You are filled with all of the anger and judgement indigenous to his character, the weight and power of his girth, the muscular structure of his arms and chest, and as you look around the room you are in through his eyes, the objects and people in the space are subject to his criticism. At this point in the process you are ready to carry this subpart into a scene in a play or film.

I had asked the actors to look at themselves in a mirror while being in that subpart they had created. The amazing thing was that in almost every instance they experienced a discernable physical difference in their face and body. I know it sounds strange and it is one of those experiences when "you had to be there," but it truly happened as I have described it. So was each actor successful in accessing the subpersonality he had asked to be there? I'm not sure that everyone had a positive experience, but I do know that several of the actors actually felt inhabited by their chosen subpart. It is just another way to focus and address eliciting our other selves.

HOW DO YOU KNOW WHEN YOU ARE REALLY INHABITED BY A SUBPERSONALITY?

Being an actor I am very familiar with the need that actors have to be successful in their performances. Whether it is working in a play or a film, the need to be "good" is always present. So quite often the psychological pusher (subpart) jumps in, and you pretend that you are inhabited by a specific subpersonality. It is a very common occurrence. I experienced it when I was originally in training with Hal and Sidra and later when I facilitated actors in voice dialogue. Faking it achieves nothing. There is absolutely nothing to gain or accomplish by pretending to be in another self.

There are specific ways to know if you are being inhabited by a subpart. You feel physically different. Your body takes on unfamiliar feelings; your muscles, posture and movements are altered in some ways. You do not feel like yourself. In some instances you feel shorter or taller, heavier or lighter. The energy is palpable. With some subparts your energy level elevates exponentially, or it goes in the opposite direction. Sometimes your body experiences a fight-or-flight reaction. When you are authentically inhabited, there is no mistaking it! The difference in how you are affected physically is also dependent on the specific energy you inhabit. For example, if you were experiencing the energy of the warrior subpart, it would be quite different from what you would feel if you were dealing with a child archetype. The physical manifestation would be very different. In any case when inhabited by another self your entire physical state would definitely be affected. You would experience feeling very different from your normal state of being.

Another way to know if you are experiencing another subpart is the way you think. The thoughts and impulses that occur are indigenous to that particular subpersonality. Every subpersonality is there to be and do what it represents. The protector-controller exists to protect and control the situation; the good father/mother is there to nourish and nurture; the vulnerable child experiences vulnerability, and so on. So if you have thoughts, impulses or commentary that goes in opposite directions and areas, it means that you are not totally inhabited by a specific subpersonality. When a subpart takes over, your entire involvement, thoughts and actions are indigenous to that specific other self. Your other selves are on this earth to do exactly what they do, and if there is any contradiction to that energy, you are not being truly inhabited by the subpart that you are trying to access.

CHAPTER 4

SUBPERSONALITIES AS AN ACTING APPROACH

THE DAILY PERSONAL SUBPERSONALITY INVENTORY

Many of my actors have accused me of packing too much work into a twenty-four-hour day. With all of the daily workout assignments suggested in all my books they feel that in order to be able to do all those things, they would need an extra ten hours to be added to each day. OK, you can be selective about the exercises and inventories you do each day. This one, however, can be done on the fly so to speak. During the sixteen hours a day when we are awake we experience many mood swings. We accept them and hardly take notice of most of the moods that occur. You should make an effort to be aware of those various feelings and moods as they come up, and you should question them.

So you suddenly feel depressed. It seems to come from nowhere. You were just finishing lunch and a heavy feeling came over you like a raincloud. That is the very moment you need to question what that feeling is and where it came from. Is it just that you are physically digesting your lunch and maybe it will pass? No, something caused it, and it might be an energy that has crept into you. So ask questions about what you are experiencing emotionally. Hypothetically, let's imagine that now, after lunch you have to go back to work and realize that the beach-bum subpart jumped in and started nagging you about not being free *(no fun, work, shit!)*. So in conjecturing terms the beach-bum subpart came into direct conflict with the disciplined responsible self, and that's what caused the depression. So instead of just shining it on, you now understand how a subpersonality can move into you and create that strong feeling of depression.

That is a single example of what you need to do when mood swings and meaningful feelings happen. Identify them; ask questions about what they mean and where they came from. Identify the physical changes in your body and the thoughts and impulses that occur. Not every emotional change that takes place in your daily activities suggests that a subpart is attempting to invade you, but by being increasingly aware of how you feel and how your emotions move through you on a moment-to-moment or hour-to-hour time frame, you will become increasingly conscious about your primary and disowned selves.

I used to jokingly say that when I was younger, I couldn't go more than a minute without a sexual thought, and now being older I can go two minutes without a sexual thought. It was my way of getting a laugh from people in my class. But some people get trapped in a sexual subpart, and without the presence of an aware ego that part stays in control and can ruin their life. Being a sexaholic is as serious a disease as being an alcoholic. But by being aware and taking daily inventory of who is there, no one needs to be trapped in a subpart. The aware ego asks the particular subpersonality to move out of the driver's seat and relinquish that position to another part. That is the job and ability of an aware ego. Many things happen in your waking day: you read the newspaper, watch television, hear about a multitude of disturbing things happening in the world; someone says something that affects you, or you argue with a co-worker. Each of those stimuli is capable of eliciting an energy that takes over. While watching a television news program, you see the horrible injustice being carried out in a small Southern town, you get angry, furious, and you feel your body shaking with rage. Let's suppose that at that very moment you elicit the trilogy of the warrior, the killer and the activist subparts. At the very moment when they enter your being, having an aware ego can deal with and control them. That is why doing a daily subpersonality inventory is so necessary; otherwise you can walk through your life in some kind of unconscious fog!

Developing an acute awareness of who is there and how they function is mandatory to understanding how your subs operate. The more familiar you become with who they are and what triggers them, the more adept you will be in your ability to access a specific subpersonality that you want to use in a scene. Suppose that you are doing a scene in a play where the character is having a meltdown. He is angry, aggressive and physically threatening to the other character. So you decide to *roleplay* yourself into a *warrior* subpersonality to address the action of the scene. Having the ability to do that is dependent on knowing who and where it is! I know it seems that you will have to take a lot of time each day to accomplish this inventory, but after a short while it will become automatic.

SUBPERSONALITIES AND ACTING

I mentioned before that when I was working with Hal Stone in the late seventies, he spoke about subpersonalities as a psychological tool but sometime later, maybe a few years, he decided that they were a process to raise consciousness. At some point I took the knowledge and experiences I was having and modified them for actors. I created multiple approaches and techniques for using subpersonalities as practical tools for addressing characters in dramatic material.

Understanding the theory behind the phenomenon of the existence of other energies, or selves, was a prerequisite to using subpersonalities as a *choice approach*. In the beginning, before translating those energies into vehicles for addressing scene obligations, I asked my students, the actors, to do voice-dialogue work with each other. As we grew aware of the subparts, and before employing them to work for us, we became very conscious that they were real, and that when they took over, they completely controlled our behavior. We learned that every subpersonality exists to be and do what it is there for.

As time passed, I asked my students to try a monologue when under the influence of a particular subpersonality. The results were amazing! The monologue, even though it was being approached irreverently, took on incredible facets and dimension. Each subpart would bring new and different colors to the same piece of material. We went from there to identifying the obligations and selecting the right subpersonality to fulfill the author's intent. Many characters in dramatic literature either live in a single subpersonality throughout the piece or go from one to another. If you can specifically select and access in you the subpersonality which happens to match the one that impels the character, you can depend on it to take you through the whole piece. What is so incredible about eliciting the help of a particular subpart is that it knows exactly how to relate and respond to the other people in each scene. It will behave just the way it has been programmed to, without commentary or redirection. Because the potential of this area is so vast and infinite, it has become a megapproach in my system. After the actor has selected the specific subpersonality, he can use one of the approach techniques to access it. In short, the subpersonality would be the *choice,* and the approach technique (voice dialogue, imaging, creating a choice to elicit the subpart, and so on) would be the *choice approach.*

While the selection of a specific subpersonality is perfect for the character in terms of his behavior and actions, it may not actually service the true reality of who he is. So while it achieves an emotional result and services the moment, it would be better to find a subpart that is a more authentic representation of the complexity of who the character is. You could access any of your selves and fulfill a multitude of obligations with a single choice and a single choice approach, whereas you would ordinarily have to make two or three selections in order to address all of your responsibilities. If you choose the right subpersonality, it will accommodate all of the character obligations, the emotional obligations, the relationship obligations, and will carry the character's sense of life, all in one fell swoop! It can greatly simplify your process, while cutting down on the number of choices and approaches you need to use in a piece.

Another important way to employ subpersonality work is to allow one of your subparts to select the choices you need in a scene or play. If, for example, you have identified the nature of the subpersonalities through which your character journeys, you can access your own parallel parts to deal with some of the other obligations of the piece. You can let those selves select choices for the time-and-place responsibilities, the thematic obligations, the various relationships the character has, and so on.

To clarify this, let us suppose that the character in this hypothetical piece has a variety of relationships with the other people in the play—his wife, his mistress, his father, his brother, and the major antagonist. His emotional point of view towards each of them is a result of which of his selves he is in when he relates to them. If you, the actor, are coming from a different energy, you might have difficulty selecting the proper parallel choices to address those relationship responsibilities. If, on the other hand, you identify from which energy the character is relating to his wife, for example, then you could elicit that subpersonality and make a much more parallel-choice selection.

Subpersonalities can also be used as a preparation. You may elect to facilitate a specific self because it makes you feel the way you want to feel *before* you start to address the demands of the material. For example, before you tackle the obligations of the first scene, you find it necessary to elevate your ego state, as well as to confront the tension and fear you feel before starting the creative process. So you decide to access the hero subpersonality, because you know that that part of you is fearless and has a positive ego. The hero subpart usually exists in the primary-self structure and is fairly easy to access. Or let us imagine that you feel the need to be more powerful. There are a number of selves whose basic superstructure is built on power: the protector, the controller, the judge, the killer, the warrior, the evangelist, the messiah, and the perfectionist, to name a few.

There are many ways to use this megapproach in your work. It is multifaceted. Before you attempt to use subpersonalities as an acting tool, however, you must first become instrumentally familiar with who your selves are, where they are, and how they function within you. By doing a lot of work exploring your instrument and using the various techniques to facilitate and bring those many subparts to the forefront, you can establish an aware ego and become familiar with all the techniques for doing so. It is then that you can begin to use this choice approach in your acting.

At this time there are thirty-one choice approaches in my system. Subpersonalities is one of the five megapproaches. Let's suppose that you are getting ready to address a character in a play or film. Let's also imagine that you want to use subpersonalities as an approach technique. Where do you begin the process?

RESEARCHING THE CHARACTER

The material provides a blueprint of sorts and can supply a lot of information about the character that you are addressing, but, maybe, not enough to feel secure about the subpersonalities that you have identified. You need to know what the impelling forces are that stimulate the character's relationships and behavior. There is so much more that you, the actor, can do to discover the complexities of each of the characters you choose to address. You can determine the character's psychological profile, for example, from all the information that you get from reading the play or screenplay: What do you learn from the specifics about his/ her emotional point of view? How does (s)he feel about society? Is there a political element involved in his/her expressions? Is (s)he conservative or liberal in his/her thinking? Is there judgement, prejudice, evident in his/her psychological structure? What effect has the environment that (s)he grew up in on his/her outlook on life? What decisions does (s)he make as a result of the impact of his/her life experience growing up in the world? At what time in history does the play take place, and what are the social mores, issues and influences that affect the character? At the time of the play what is the world experiencing? depression and economic deprivation? political restrictions? All of those realities have a meaningful impact on what subpersonalities the character might be impelled by.

The development of personality is very dependent on environment and parental influences. The primary selves are created and evolve as a result of many of the issues and realities that exist in the very early years of a child. We all go through a variety of damaging experiences, particularly in our early years. They create a need to develop protections and insulations against that damage. Almost everyone has a protector subpart; the pleaser also develops at an early age, as well as a few others, depending on the nature of the damaging experiences. My last book, *A Second Chance at Life,* describes the many ways we are damaged and how to repair that damage. It might be valuable to use it in relation to researching and interpreting characters you need to address.

How far and how deep you journey into the researching of a character is up to you. I said that I was going to demystify the subpersonality process and hopefully not complicate it; however, you should be open to discovering anything that comes up for you while exploring the character.

Continuing with the research, you might do some *active imagination* with the character you are addressing. Starting with everything you know about him, you talk to him or her, asking for responses. Those responses are largely dependent on your imagination.

Let us imagine that you are speaking to Tom Wingfield in *The Glass Menagerie*, for example: *Tom, how do you feel about your life at the moment? How do you feel about your job at the warehouse? What would you rather be doing if you had a choice? How do you feel about your sister, your mother, the apartment you live in?* and so on. You allow for him to respond to each of your questions. So many of them are based on what you already know, but you might be surprised at the responses you get. Those unexpected responses could give you a greater understanding of how he feels and where he is. What if you employed active imagination with Laura and Amanda? Do you think that you might achieve a greater understanding of the play and what each of the characters is really like? Active imagination is also a valuable technique that you can use to explore your dreams, understand who is in them and what they want.

The exploration can be much easier if you are playing a character based on a real person. You have a tremendous amount of information about that person, which would almost always lead you to the right subpersonality choices. A very good example would be the character in the film *Citizen Kane,* which was based on William Randolph Hearst, the publishing tycoon. Hearst had a media empire, twenty daily newspapers and eleven Sunday papers in thirteen cities. He controlled the King Features Syndicate and the International News Service as well as six magazines, including Cosmopolitan, Good Housekeeping and Harper's Bazaar. This indeed was an empire at a time of financial hardships for the common person. When the film went into production, knowing it would be a critical portrayal of him, Hearst attempted to stop it from being made. I'm happy that he failed to do so! He had enormous power and influence in important places. It is rumored that he shot and killed a man on his yacht over an argument about the women he was involved with. It never became public but was covered up, and he was never prosecuted. That is the kind of power he had in the world! If the actor (Orson Welles) playing him were to approach the role using subpersonalities, the knowledge of his life would be extremely helpful in choosing the right subparts. The character is obviously motivated by an obsessive achiever and dictator subpersonality. He is driven to achieve and accomplish his obsessive goals. Because of his phenomenal success, he becomes dictatorial with all the people in his life. If an actor were to play a character like this one, it would be a great advantage for him to explore using subpersonalities. POWER would definitely be one of the first choices. The controller, perfectionist and dictator subparts would also come into play. Once inhabited by the right choices, all the actor would need to do is get out of the way of the subparts he had elicited.

Many plays and films have been written where the character is someone you know about, for example the artist Vincent van Gogh. I have a twelve-hundred-page book on his life! So if I were to play him, I would have the entire story of his life to pick from: his childhood, his involvement with art, his relationships, his psychological profile, his obsessions and his mental states. There would be an incredible blueprint to follow, specific behaviors that illuminate a thought process, emotional priorities, and so on. Selecting the impelling subparts that were in control at specific times of his life would be the work that I would have to do to inhabit the correct subpersonality. Going from one subpart to another would depend on creating an aware ego that would enable me to make the changes.

Let us examine another character, somewhat more complicated, Pablo Picasso. The big difference in this artist's life as opposed to Van Gogh's was the fact that he was very successful, very famous and very rich as a result of his visibility in the world. Vincent only sold one painting in his entire life, and that was to his brother Theo. Picasso was also a political activist, a man with an enormous libido, a huge ego and probably a misguided idea of being physically attractive. His painting of *Guernica* in 1937 is one of his best-known works. It is regarded by many art critics as one of the most powerful antiwar paintings in history. The canvas covers a complete wall in the Reina Sofia Museum in Madrid. I am so proud that I personally have seen it. It was created by Picasso to express his outrage over the bombing of a Basque city in Northern Spain by the Nazis, who were supporting General Franco. This black-and-white painting has become an international symbol of genocide committed during war time. An interesting incident occurred in relation to it: In the 1940s a Nazi officer who was visiting Picasso's studio in Paris asked him, "You did this?" Picasso's response was, "No, *you* did!" With all of this information, the actor addressing the character would have enough to be able to select the right subpersonalities.

There are so many other characters in dramatic literature that an actor could research in order to create their many facets. Take Lincoln, for example. Daniel Day-Lewis played him in the film that was recently made. There are probably dozens of biographical books, papers, stories about our fifteenth president. On an interview I saw, Day-Lewis said he worked to get his voice; it was high-pitched and had a specific tone that he wanted to embody. I really don't know if he knew anything about subpersonality work, or if in fact he did not elicit a subpart, even by accident. However, it would be possible to do so using the many techniques that are available.

So many biopics have been made over the years. *Patton* is a World War II film about the life and exploits of the famous and controversial general. MacArthur was another historical general who has been depicted as difficult and often described as a "warmonger." He was fired by President Truman because he wanted to bomb the supply lines feeding the North Koreans in that war. In order to accomplish that he would have had to cross into Chinese territories, and Truman did not want to bring China into the war! But, listen to a private first class's (me) theory about that whole thing: It was the right decision for any West Point graduate to have made: Cut the head off the snake, and the snake will die! Some of the other biopics made had to do with Capote, Steve Jobs, Howard Hughes, Jackie Robinson, Ludwig van Beethoven, Jerry Lee Lewis, Jimi Hendricks, Nixon, Lou Gehrig, and so many more.

Let us suppose, on the other hand, that you are going to address a character that isn't famous but is an average unknown person in the world. Where do you begin your research? Of course, you start with the script and digest all the information offered by the material. Then you must explore the character obligation. There are four parts to it: what is the character like physically, emotionally, intellectually and psychologically? Start with questions: What kind of person is (s)he? What is his/her physical makeup? Is (s)he physically fit, frail? Is (s)he attractive? Is (s)he mentally stable or unstable? What is his/her level of intelligence, consciousness? What is his/her temperament? Is (s)he mellow or volatile? Is (s)he suspicious by nature, paranoid? Is s(he) bright? All of those factors have direct bearing on how the character relates to life. Once you have answered all of the questions, you must ask yourself, How am I like this character and how am I unlike him/her? All of your answers will take you to the work that you must do to inhabit this person. And hopefully it will clarify what subpersonalities are motivating and impelling him/her to behave and relate. Then you must address the historical obligation of the piece, the time in history that the character is living in. Identify all of the issues that he is experiencing. Go to the historical obligation, and begin your exploration there. In my system there are seven major obligations that exist in any material, and the actor must address those in a specific play or film (in my book *Irreverent Acting*, all seven are listed and described). Again, you must become familiar with all of the elements that exist in that time and place.

THE HISTORICAL OBLIGATION

This obligation area relates to the time in history in which the film or play takes place. It could mean any period in history. If the actor hired to play a character isn't familiar with the period, then he must research it thoroughly. He must become familiar with the customs, morality, mores, concerns, economics, laws, rules, etiquette, politics, dress, sexual attitudes, awareness, and consciousness of the people of that time and geographical locale. All of those realities must be dealt with when relating to a time other than the contemporary period. The actor should draw parallels with the present whenever possible and find the contrasts so that he can experience the components of the past.

The investigative process almost always starts with questions: What were the weather conditions? the climate? How did that affect the people's behavior? What were the language and speech patterns? the mannerisms? What was the people's psychological awareness? religion? How did religion, superstition and rituals influence their lives? How did they feel about birth and death? What was the life expectancy of the period?

You could go on almost indefinitely asking and answering those kinds of questions. All those elements have an impact on how the character looks at life, how he relates to people, speaks, thinks, acts, walks and talks. Before an actor can deal with anything else, such as the emotional obligation or the relationship obligation, he must understand and confront the various historic obligations that relate to the specific period that the character is involved with. When creating the various elements of the past using any choice or choice approach, it is entirely possible to access many sub-personalities. Every period in time brings with it issues that affect, preoccupy and impel the behavior of a character.

Let us go through a few periods to illustrate the point:

Greek drama: All of their plays were about high-born people: kings, the Olympian gods, Orestes, Agamemnon, Electra, or Cassandra. Their plays did not deal with or address the common man, who was not worthy of tragedy.

Elizabethan theater: It dealt with tragedies, comedies and characters like Hamlet, Macbeth, or Othello.

The Restoration: Almost every play dealt with or addressed cuckolding! They were preoccupied with women cheating and cuckolding their husbands. The husband's response and actions totally related to the subject.

In each of those periods there was a theme and a preoccupation with power, ambition and revenge. Each brought with it great emphasis on the human condition and how the people coped with the circumstances of their lives. Let us imagine that there existed great strife, war, hunger and disease, for example. The subpersonalities that would develop in such circumstances would be *the victim, survivor,* and *protector* energies. If indeed all of our primary selves are created to protect the vulnerable child and some of the other child archetypes, then the subparts that would be created would fall into the category of protection and survival.

I would like to concentrate on three separate periods in American history: the time of the Great Depression, from 1929 to 1941, the period of the Second World War, 1941 to 1945, and as the third period the post-war years in America, 1945 to 1959.

THE GREAT DEPRESSION

In the years of the Depression, the plays and films dealt with the economic pressures of society. Millions were out of work; it was like an economic pandemic! There were bread lines and soup kitchens to feed the people who had nothing to eat. The period was called the Great Depression and that is what most people experienced, depression. Almost all the plays and some of the films dealt with the impact of deprivation, of being able to survive.

The Plays and Films of That Time

Winterset, a play by Maxwell Anderson, was one of the most important plays written in verse. It was written in 1935 during the Depression, and it dealt with the famous Sacco-Vanzetti case, which involved two Italian immigrants with radical beliefs who were arrested, prosecuted and executed for conspiracy to commit a crime against America. It was a time in our country when there was a great deal of animosity and hatred against immigrants.

The Grapes of Wrath, written by John Steinbeck, details the hardships of agricultural workers who picked vegetables and fruit from the fields. During the

Depression there was a drought in Middle America that caused the dust bowl, when all of those workers moved west hoping to find work in other climates. Their struggle to survive is what the novel is all about. Steinbeck wrote several novels with similar themes: *East of Eden, Tortilla Flats, Cannery Row, Sweet Thursday,* and many more. While some of his books were written after the Depression, many of the themes are very similar.

Awake and Sing, by Clifford Odets, was produced on Broadway in 1935. *Waiting for Lefty* was another Depression play of Odets'. The films of the period dealt with the impact of the Depression, and the characters in those films were affected and impelled by the realities of the period, films such as *The Public Enemy, I Am a Fugitive from a Chain Gang,* and others that dealt honestly with the tragedy of the Depression. And then there were the escape and fantasy films, the Marx Brothers' *Duck Soup, The Wizard of Oz, It Happened One Night, Snow White and the Seven Dwarfs* and *Fantasia,* films that were aimed at distracting people from their misery.

So if an actor was going to address a character from the Depression period he would need to create choices that would stimulate emotional responses paralleling that time period. By doing that he would be more available to experiencing the various subpersonalities that would be elicited as a result of creating a sense of that time and place. Those subparts might range from the victim to the protector, survivor, and the spiritual energies that might be elicited by the need to turn to God for rescue. And if the character is involved with distracting himself from the pain, the actor could be affected by accessing the child archetypes, such as the imaginative-child or the magical-child energy.

THE SECOND WORLD WAR YEARS

After the attack on Pearl Harbor, which signaled the end of the Great Depression, our country went into high gear, putting people to work by the tens of thousands and creating fervor in America unlike anything I have personally ever seen. It brought us together on a level that was deep and meaningful! The plays and films at the time were patriotic and inspiring, demonizing the enemy and showcasing great acts of heroism. The only other time in the history of our country when I experienced a similar cohesion between the people was during the Kennedy years. So the subpersonalities elicited during those years were likely to be the hero, patriot and warrior subparts. Even though people were being killed and the horror of war had its casualties, on the home front people were loving, hopeful and kind to each other. An actor playing a character from that period needs to research it and find in himself those subparts that impelled the behavior of the people at that time.

THE POST-WAR YEARS

They too were years of hope and reconstruction, of rebuilding society and moving into areas of art and creativity. The plays and films of that period were some of the best that came out of Hollywood: soldiers coming home and reestablishing relationships with their loved ones, returning to work, rebuilding their lives after the years of the horror of war. By the beginning of the 1950s the vitality of American theater was acknowledged around the world. Some of the films of that time were *The Best Years of Our Lives, Death of a Salesman, The Crucible, A Streetcar Named Desire, Cat on a Hot Tin Roof, All My Sons* and many others. It was also a dark period with McCarthyism, HUAC and a hysterical hunt for Communists in our country. Arthur Miller, Tennessee Williams, and Eugene O'Neill were writing meaningful plays that went into the depth and meaning of life. The characters were complex and dimensional. It was a time when the actor had the opportunity to explore the depths of emotional life and the real meaning of relationships. By exploring this period of plays and films, he can look for and find the energies that drove the behavior of the characters in them.

SOME EXAMPLES OF CHARACTERS TO ADDRESS

You begin by reading the play or screenplay and looking for all of the information provided by the author. It is almost like being an acting detective. Start by asking questions: What does the author say about the character? What does the character say about himself? What does he say to the other characters in the piece? What do the other characters say about him? What are his actions throughout the piece? Can you identify a specific energy, a quality of behavior that has a tangible and identifiable emotional sameness to it? Apply all of the research that you have done related to the character and use all of the discoveries garnered by that research. After doing all of that you should have a pretty good idea of what subpart is impelling the character's behavior. At that point you begin the process of accessing that part of you.

Let us take as an example Laura in *The Glass Menagerie*. The main subpersonalities that impel her are the *shy child,* the *frightened child* and the *dreamer.* There is also some *victim* energy in her. So where do you begin? Let us suppose that at first you are nowhere near to any of those energies. So you start the process of accessing the *shy child* by looking for a choice that will stimulate it. In other words, in this case the approach technique for accessing the subpart is using choices. You can create that choice using sense memory as a technique. It could be an event or experience you had.

OK, but for the sake of the lesson, let us say that that approach doesn't work. You have to try one of the other ways to access the shy child. So you try to roleplay yourself into that energy. Having explored all of the approach techniques for accessing subpersonalities, you are familiar with where that subpart is, and knowing that, you walk into that energy. Once you are inhabited by it, you can begin to move into some of the other child archetypes. The lonely child can lead you into the magical child, and that in turn can excite and elicit the dreamer. Once you are totally inhabited by a subpersonality, there is very little else that you need to do. The relationships and action of the play affect each of the subpersonalities that Laura (you) is experiencing.

A personal note here: in my childhood years there were many things or objects that I had and used: I spent a lot of time with a yoyo and became quite good with it. I had penny candy, spinning tops and a paddle with a ball attached to it that I kept hitting, hoping that I didn't miss. I would also roller-skate on the street, ride my bike, listen to the radio after school and engage in a host of other activities. If I created those objects and activities, they would take me back to my childhood and help to access the subparts. The actor playing Laura could do the same thing, going back to objects from childhood, re-creating them and allowing that involvement to take her wherever it does.

Even before you decide to address a subpersonality that you have identified as right for the character, it would be wise to understand what the stimulus is that created the subparts the character is in. Laura, for instance, is shy and asocial because she accepts that she is crippled, and that makes her want to hide from public view. Several of the child archetypes are acting in concert with each other here: the vulnerable child, the shy child, the lonely child, and the frightened child. Laura goes in and out each of them and finds ways to preoccupy herself in fantasy. The actor can address that a number of ways: She can work to create environments from her own childhood, hoping to access the child energies, or she can create objects that appeal to her inner child. For the insecurity and the victim energy, she can use specific events of her life, and in rehearsing to play the part she should explore the many avenues available to her. That is what rehearsals are for.

Another example is Gordon Gekko in *Wall Street,* a character driven by ambition and greed. He is self-involved and self-serving, with little concern for anyone else except for how they might be exploited for his selfish needs. His acquisitions never seem enough; there is always a need for more. In psychological terms what do you think would create this kind of personality? Where does this hunger for material wealth and power come from? The obvious conclusion is intense fear and insecurity, a lack of self-esteem and entitlement, growing up as a child in an environment of deprivation, lack of acceptance and visibility and a need to beg and struggle for every necessity—food, shelter, privacy and love. So where does an actor go to start exploring his own life? What are the experiences he had growing up that might elicit the ambition and the greed for all of the material objects that would quell the agonizing need to overcome the unconscious impact of all those damaging experiences? Wow, this is a tough one, particularly if the actor doesn't relate to the sources or origins that might have produced a Gordon Gekko.

OK, let us assume that I, Eric Morris, have been cast in the remake of that film. I'm an actor, in training since 1950 and certainly experienced enough to address any role, right? Maybe not! Looking back at my life, one would think that it was blessed! I was the last of five children; all of my siblings were much older than I, with my oldest brother twenty years older, and the closest in age, my sister Helen, almost twelve years older. Even though I was born in the time of the Great Depression, I never wanted for anything. I knew that my parents loved me, and my siblings indulged me for the most part. My mother had already raised four children and was very tired, so she turned the responsibility for mothering and raising me over to my sister Ida, who was seventeen years my senior.

So where can I go, what can I draw on to address Gordon's avaricious greed and self-involvement? Well at this point one would think that if I was going to play this part I would have no underpinnings to build on. So if I accept the role, do I have to fake it? NO! Let's *selectively emphasize* the other parts of my life:

None of the members of my family ever expected anything from me. I was just the blue-eyed, blond kid who was the little brother. My sister Ida was so protective of me that she turned me into an awkward kid who had no physical abilities or prowess. She was always saying things like: "Be careful; you'll fall," or "Don't climb on that; you will hurt yourself!" I always felt that I could not catch up to my older siblings, no matter how fast I would run. Grade school and high school were a nightmare. I didn't do well. It was hard for me to understand things. In sports I was always the last one to be chosen to be on a team, and even accepting me was greeted with reluctance. I have never really, and to this day, learned to read properly. My eighth-grade teacher, Miss Lane, wanted to hold me back for another year, keeping me from graduating because, as she told my brothers, who had gone to the principal to protest her decision, I was "intellectually challenged" and could not keep up with the others. She felt that I should go to a technical high school and learn a trade, something that I could do with my hands to eventually earn a living. And if I agreed to do that, she added, she would let me graduate with my class. I mentioned earlier how I was one of the only two Jewish kids in my neighborhood, which was filled with anti-Semites, and as a result I was bullied and physically abused. Going to school every day was like living in a freakish nightmare. When the bell rang at the end of a school day, I had to run like lightning to avoid getting beat up. I had to graduate from high school in summer school because I couldn't keep up with all my subjects in the last year, so I did not graduate with my class. I dropped out of the first semester of college and went to work in a factory making children's phonographs. My two brothers were so alarmed that I was working on a drill press that they sent me to a psychologist to get some much needed therapy. After a year with Doctor Ruby Segal, I became aware that my inabilities scholastically and physically had their source in my feeling unable to compete with my much older siblings. As a result, I had made myself incapable in order to justify that reality. Even as I write this, I am feeling anger and resentment rising up in my body. I feel the need to show all of them who I am, what I can do, and what I have accomplished! I truly believe that I was driven to show my family and all of the abusers that I would surpass them all in the level of success that I have achieved.

So there you have it! I can access a subpersonality that would take me into the thrust and behavior of a Gordon Gekko type of character. Even when you hit a wall and feel so far from the character and a subpersonality, don't despair, because you can selectively emphasize your own personal realities to find an impetus that will take you to the subpersonality that you are attempting to elicit. Fortunately, I have been very successful in my life, and by the grace of the God energy and thanks to Doctor Segal, I was able to graduate from college in the upper five percent of my class.

Let's breakdown the specific process involved in addressing the Gordon Gekko character: The controller, the pusher and the perfectionist subparts are the most obvious with which to begin your exploration. As you venture into it you may discover that there are more subpersonalities that might pop up in rehearsals. So what are the techniques you might use to elicit those other selves? I used my own life, *selectively emphasizing* the areas that would stimulate the rebellion and access the proper subparts. You could explore the following approach techniques to see where they take you and whether they really create the life and behavior of the Gekko character:

1. Selectively emphasizing personal realities
2. Using an external, possibly a predatory animal
3. Using a person that is like the character
4. Roleplaying

The television newscaster in the film *Network* is another interesting example that we can use to explore subpersonalities. He has that famous monologue that ends with, "Go to your window, open it up, and shout, I'm mad as hell and I'm not going to take it anymore!" He is definitely fed up with what is going on in the country—the corruption and government control, the propaganda and the violation of human rights, and so on. Peculiarly, at this writing we are in the most tragic situation I have ever experienced in my almost ninety years of living. We are experiencing a global pandemic that is killing hundreds of thousands of people all over the world, an epidemic that spreads like a wild, uncontrollable fire without a cure in sight, with a political administration run by a psychopathic president who fuels the fires of discontent and division and who has been credited with telling over ten thousand lies to the American people. Massive protests are going on right now against the killing of a black man by four police officers. The streets all over America are filled with thousands of people in spite of their possible exposure to the pandemic. The incredible number of violations of civil rights against African Americans by law enforcement has been going on for decades!

So with the entire *available stimulus* present, the actor addressing the newscaster's character in *Network* has a plethora of personal realities to draw from. The subpersonalities might be the activist, the revolutionary and the patriot.

1. Here again there are enough available stimuli to use the actor's personal realities and point of view. He can do a sharing monologue to himself, to an empty room or standing in the street, reiterating all of the available stimuli and truths that are actively occurring at this time.

2. He might also explore all of the things about being an American that are important to him,

reminding himself of all the wonderful things that our country stands for: the Constitution, Abraham Lincoln, the Bill of Rights, the Thirteenth Amendment, etc.

3. He might play music, patriotic marches. They work for me!

There are so many characters in plays and films that are impelled by subpersonalities, and once the actor discovers and inhabits those other selves he can achieve experiential success.

OTHER CHARACTERS IN DRAMATIC MATERIAL THAT CAN BE IMPELLED BY A SUBPERSONALITY

An entire book can be written about the multitude of characters in plays and films that are impelled by the energies of subpersonalities. All of the examples in this section are my suggestions as to what subparts might be used to stimulate and impel the characters' behavior. When reading this section, imagine yourself doing all of these characters. Allow yourself to actually explore your own subpersonalities that are parallel to each of the ones discussed. It is a valuable practice and it teaches you how to identify subs in characters and how to elicit them.

A number of years ago I directed the play, *'Night Mother,* a two-character play that has no intermissions, so that the action that takes place is uninterrupted. The character Jessie (the daughter) announces to her mother (the other character) that she is going to kill herself in the next two hours. From that point on she tries to explain to her mother why she has made that decision, while her mother attempts to change her mind. In the beginning the actress playing Jessie should be in a victim subpart and should move between that part and the loving responsible daughter. Since she has been totally responsible for taking care of her mother, she must now teach her about all the things that must be done to run the house: how to pay bills, whom to contact in emergencies and a plethora of other involvements. The action and the emotions in the relationship are extremely intense. As the play continues, there are three potential subpersonalities the actress playing Jessie needs to explore: First, the victim, because Jessie spends a lot of time explaining why she has decided on suicide, talking about her unfulfilled life, all of her disappointments, the fact that her son is a thief and a criminal and that she is prone to having grand-mal seizures as a result of epilepsy. Second, since Jessie is also obligated to preparing her mother to exist without her, the actress must move into another subpart: the loving and responsible daughter. And third, when Jessie ultimately does in fact leave the room and kill herself, the transition should probably come from a controller subpart. The responsibility of the actor is to be able to transition from one subpersonality to another and to have the techniques available to successfully make those transitions. This is where the eleventh level of consciousness comes in and makes it possible to establish awareness so the transitions can be accomplished.

In my direction of the play I helped the actress to select choices that hopefully would access those specific subpersonalities. Whatever the result was, we had a very successful run of the play, and both actors were magnificent in their performances.

In Sam Shepard's play *Fool for Love,* Eddie and May are obsessively sexually and emotionally tied to each other. It is almost impossible for them to be apart. Their sexual obsession controls their lives and is the major impetus of their relationship. In the action of the play it is discovered that they are half-brother and sister, both of them having the same father but different mothers, which might explain the genetic elements that create the obsession. There are complex facets to their relationship, and while the obvious subparts to be explored would be the Don Juan and Aphrodite subpersonalities, there is a bond between them that goes beyond their sexual attachment to each other. Could it be another subpart or can it be an additional element in the Don Juan and Aphrodite energies? In reality, if we were to explore all of our sexual experiences, wouldn't we feel that specific ones went beyond the normal sexual attraction and needs? I personally know of someone, who shall remain anonymous, whose life was almost ruined by an Eddie and May kind of relationship. So what was it in that particular relationship that created the obsession? My conclusion is that the approach to the Don Juan and Aphrodite subparts needs to explore the various elements and complexities of those sexual subpersonalities. What was it that was so different in the sexual relationship that my friend had with his partner that produced the obsessive ingredients? I believe that is what must be explored by the two actors playing Eddie and May. It may also mean that the actors need to find a second subpersonality that would intensify the impact of Don Juan and Aphrodite.

Othello is the warrior and then the victim and then the killer, and that is the way the action of the play is structured. The actor approaching this role might start rehearsing by elevating his ego and having a powerful self-image. Quite often it is a liability to jump too quickly into a subpart. When the actor feels ready to work to elicit the warrior subpart, he should stay inhabited with that energy until the action of the play demands a meaningful change into a different energy and another subpersonality. So when Iago begins to instill Othello with suspicion about his wife's disloyalty, the actor must move into the victim subpart, and finally when he is convinced of her betrayal, he accesses the killer and kills her. In relation to selecting and accessing subpersonalities this role is rather simple. Quite often it is the content of a piece of material that in itself is impacting enough to elicit the next subpart.

In playing Romeo, it would be simplistic to say that the actor could go back and forth between his romantic child-adult and his Don Juan subparts. We must not forget that *Romeo and Juliet* is one of Shakespeare's tragedies. What makes it a tragedy is that two young people who are deeply in love with each other are not able to come together because of their feuding families. How must the actor playing Romeo address this element of the play? Does he move into his vulnerable child-adult subpart? Or is there another self the actor should explore? If so, what other energy does he look for? Is it the confused child-adult subpersonality or the rebellious one? I am making a point of combining child and adult subparts because Romeo and Juliet are teenagers. Finally, when Romeo dies and Juliet drinks the poison, what subpersonality must the actress playing her call forth? There are a lot of questions the actor must explore and find the answers to. To me, the excitement and joy of acting reside in the journey to discover the stimulus that impels the actor to find the right subpersonalities that take him into actually experiencing the realities.

Hamlet is another complex character and a very young man. So many actors, some in their sixties, have attempted to play him. The reality is that he is seventeen years old, not quite an adult. When I was studying acting at Northwestern University, I was about twenty-two. I was fascinated by the role and intimidated by my lack of training and exposure to Shakespeare, so I embarked on doing pieces of the play, monologues and soliloquies, in my acting classes. I could do several of his monologues, but since I knew so little of the craft, I was only able to understand some of what he was experiencing. Almost seventy years later in retrospect, I understand why it is so difficult for a seventeen-year-old actor to address this character. There are so many things that Hamlet experiences in the play. There is a whole list of subpersonalities that an actor approaching this character could explore and attempt to inhabit, such as the child-archetype subpersonalities—the vulnerable child, the hurt child, the abused child-adult and the rebellious child-adult—as well as the victim sub-part, the cunning achiever, the hero, and the warrior-killer. The selections depend on the action of the play as it evolves. In the beginning Hamlet is confused and vulnerable. He feels like a victim, but when his father's ghost appears, it changes everything. He begins to contemplate actions he must take. From that point on the actor approaching this role must use the given circumstances and the evolution of the play to decide on which subpersonality he must address.

Felix, the character in the play *The Odd Couple,* is influenced by a cornucopia of subpersonalities. Some of them work in tandem with each other. His pusher and perfectionist team up and are active throughout the play. In some of the later scenes he moves into the responsible self and later, when dealing with Oscar, who is kicking him out of his apartment, he displays his judgmental self. The actor playing Felix must know where and when to activate those energies. He must use one or more of the ten techniques to access the subpart that he needs. The actor can roleplay himself into the pusher and perfectionist subparts by suggesting them to himself and walking into the energies of both. When an actor is dealing with two personalities inhabiting him at the same time, the subparts move back and forth in him. Being successful with sub-personality work is very dependent on knowing that those subparts exist and where they are. That is why doing subpersonality inventory on a daily basis is so important.

In *A Doll's House* by Henrik Ibsen, Nora, one of the leading characters, is controlled by her husband,

Torvald, who has dictatorial influence over everything she does. She is the doll in the doll's house. The actress exploring this role probably starts with the obedient-wife subpersonality and goes back and forth between that and a victim subpart. As the play proceeds, Nora begins to come into the awareness of her relationship with Torvald, and at that point she moves into the rebellious-wife energy and stands up for herself. There is room here for the actress to access the power and hero subpersonalities. Towards the end of the play Nora walks out of the house and slams the door, and that was the door slam that was heard all around the world! You might think of it as the beginning of the women's liberation movement. For the most part in every play or film the character's behavior and actions make it clear what subpersonalities the actor should look for.

In the movie *Rain* the main character is a reverend and a very pious moralist who is determined to save the soul of a prostitute. It is a very old film, shot in 1932. Walter Huston and Joan Crawford were the actors in it. The actor playing the preacher can quickly identify the subpart that is most obvious in his behavior and relationship to the woman. It is the Martin Luther subpersonality that is the thrust of all of his actions and behavior. His relationship to the prostitute is driven with the fervor of his intense moral obligation to save her from burning in Hell. As it turns out, the prostitute seduces the preacher, who ends up having sex with her. So it seems that the actor must move from a Martin Luther into a Don Juan subpersonality.

It is easy to identify the two different subparts and to access them.

It is important at this juncture to talk about finding the multifarious subpersonalities in us. What if, for example, the actor approaching the character of the preacher in *Rain* cannot find that subpersonality in himself? I believe that we all have primary and disowned subpersonalities that could fulfill all of the emotional obligations of every dramatic character ever created. We must not be so literal about any specific subpersonality we need to elicit. As an example, the preacher in *Rain* is a staunch moralist, so the Martin Luther subpart is an accurate choice for him. However, even though you or I do not have such a stringent moralistic subpart, we do have feelings of right and wrong, many of which relate to a sense of what is morally correct. So if we were to address that role, we might look for the part of our personality that houses that element of morality and encourage it to take the forefront in our behavior, and instead of calling it the Martin Luther subpart, we can rename it the moralist.

A number of years ago at my theater in Hollywood, I directed one of my favorite plays, *The Glass Menagerie*, by Tennessee Williams. I spent almost a year doing it. I am including it in this section because I can point out the various subpersonalities that exist in three of the characters in the play, Amanda, Laura, and Tom. Amanda is the mother of the other two. Tom is the older son and Laura the younger daughter. I don't know if it is common knowledge, but the play is an autobiographical account of Williams's life and family. It is different from all of his other works.

Taking each character one at a time, and starting with Amanda, we can say that she experiences a variety of subpersonalities. She is a responsible-good mother, particularly in relation to her daughter, Laura, who is physically handicapped. She is a demanding bad mother in relation to Tom, whom she holds responsible for keeping the family financially above water. She has a very strong protector-controller energy and moves in and out of the responsible mother. She also has a very powerful critic, which she accesses in relation to Tom.

She loves both her children, but is in desperate living circumstances. Laura is not capable of functioning in the world, which is of great concern to Amanda. What's to become of Laura if she doesn't meet someone and marry, or learn a skill so that she eventually can take care of herself? The actress's responsibility in moving from one subpart into another is dependent on the action of the play. The techniques for making those changes can be rehearsed and triggers acquired, such as sensory suggestions, specific choices, available stimulus, and so on.

I have already talked about Laura in an earlier section. She wears a brace on one of her legs, which is shorter than the other, so she thinks of herself as a cripple, and the main subpersonalities she is impelled by are the shy child, the frightened child and the dreamer. She loves her mother and her brother. She has created a story and a fantasy life for each of her glass figures, which stand on a small table in the living room, and she spends much of every day playing and fantasizing about each one. A side note here: when I was directing the play, and because I believe there should be no acting in acting, I had the actress, Erin Nico, pick all of the glass animals herself and only the ones that resonated with her. We walked down Hollywood Boulevard and stopped at every store that had little glass figures. I felt that if Erin selected them, they would already have a life that she could build on. In the rehearsals I had her share her fantasies about each figure with the other actors.

Tom is quite complex. He is very frustrated working in a shoe factory, while desperately wanting to go out into the world and have adventures. He is concerned and responsible for Laura, whom he loves, and has a lot of resentment toward his demanding and critical mother. So his subpersonalities are the dreamer, the good son/the bad son, the rebellious son, and the responsible loving brother. In the play Tom is fired from his job at the shoe factory for writing a poem on the lid of a shoe box and I suppose for other inadequacies on the job. In rehearsal I had the actor playing Tom actually write poetry and read it to all of us. I think that after a while he wrote some pretty good poems.

All of the actors in the play had other choices that they dealt with in the confines of the material. As a rule, all of the other choices must be selected from within a subpersonality. When an actor is in a subpart, it is that energy that impels his or her behavior, so selecting choices outside of the influence of that subpart would come into conflict with the efficacy of the character in it. During some of our rehearsal time I would relate to the actors, facilitating each of them into the emotional areas that I wanted him or her to experience. It wasn't voice dialogue as such, but I do feel that it did take them into what I believe were subpersonalities.

CHAPTER 5

THE MULTIPLE FACETS OF SUBPERSONALITIES

EXPLORING THE MULTIPLE FACETS OF A SUBPERSONALITY

I know that the following statement has been made by Hal Stone in his books and by me at least a dozen times, but it bears repeating: **Every subpersonality only exists to do what it is supposed to do!** That is why it exists. Interesting concept and promoted for decades, it is, however, simplistic, and in need of exploration and defining. Let's take the *Don Juan* subpart for example. It is the male sexual subpersonality, but what kind of sexuality? romantic sexuality? animal, primal sexuality? kinky sexuality? If an actor accesses the Don Juan subpart, what sexual component is he experiencing?

Let's take another example, the killer subpersonality. What kind of energy does it contain? Is it someone protecting another person from being harmed? Is it involved in an act of self-defense or is it a cold-blooded killer who enjoys killing? You might say that it depends on the circumstance that the actor finds himself in, what the scene calls for. It would also be easy to say that the content of every subpart can be influenced by accessing another subpart to intervene. That would be a handy answer to preserve the logic and status-quo of our beliefs in the efficacy of each of our subpersonalities. It certainly would make things easier to accept! But no, I believe that this issue needs to be explored, experimented with and defined. Every person is as individual as his fingerprints, so wouldn't it make sense that each of our subpersonalities too carries within it our specific "fingerprint"? Or can it also be that the content of each subpart is subject to moving from one emotional place to another, and if so what are the mechanics of making those adjustments while under the influence of a specific subpart? There are a lot of questions to be answered here! In essence, is each of our subpersonalities indigenous to us specifically—yes, no? It shines a light on subpersonality work in a new way, doesn't it?

Once this concept occurred to me it rolled around in my brain for some time. Even as I conducted my subpersonality jamborees and was faithful to all of the original precepts, I was bothered by the notion that a subpart can have numerous facets. I know it is a theory, but isn't it possible that the original archetype where a subpersonality comes from can contain more and embody more than one aspect of behavior? In the original approach, each subpart is there to do what it is meant to do, and when another one presents itself to be recognized, the actor/person embraces it. Well, my theory is that it is not another subpart but just another facet of the original one.

I experimented with my ideas by roleplaying myself into a number of different subpersonalities, and when doing that I suggested a different impetus to enter the circumstance, and as a result, each of the subparts that I was in at the time took on other elements of behavior. I did this with a large number of subpersonalities and came to the conclusion that my theory was valid. That is not to say that it doesn't need further exploration. Our fingerprints are unique to each of us, our DNA is an imprint of individuality, our genetic blueprint is also unique in its description of who we are, so doesn't it make sense that our subpersonalities function in similar ways?

I consulted the Internet and borrowed the following section from there:

In 1921 a Swiss psychologist named Hermann Rorschach created a test aimed at determining whether there were abnormalities in a person's personality. It was clear that his test measured disordered thinking, for example as found in schizophrenia. It is also often used in determining the mental state of a criminal in the justice system, and many psychologists employ it to gauge personality and emotional stability, even though there has been a lot of debate as to its accuracy and dependability and on how useful it might be. Except for how accurately it can diagnose schizophrenia, the list for what it fails to diagnose includes depression, anxiety disorders, psychopathic personality and violent criminal tendencies.

"The Rorschach test is a psychological test in which subjects' perceptions of inkblots are recorded and then analyzed using psychological interpretation, complex algorithms, or both. Some psychologists use this test to examine a person's personality characteristics and emotional functioning." (Wikipedia)

So, conjecturing, is a serial rapist trapped in some kind of a distorted Don Juan energy? Or is a sexaholic equally trapped in a sexual energy that behaves relentlessly, every moment, obsessing about sex? Are serial killers, in the killer subpart, also embodying demonic facets? How many facets, or what other elements can each of our subpersonalities contain? Those are important queries that must take place in order for us to truly understand our subpersonalities and how to employ them as a megapproach.

The reason I am relating that quote and information is to make some important points related to subpersonalities. When people taking the Rorschach test are asked what they see in those inkblots, they describe them in various ways that depend on how they see the figures in them. It is truly a personal interpretation of their view of life, of the world, of their relationship to other people, their distortions of reality, and so on, whereas in reality they are just looking at patterns of inkblots. It is an expression of their mental state and unconscious feelings being expressed through what they say they see in the inkblots.

So for our exploration purposes, let's suppose you access a subpart such as the protector or the controller, and hypothetically that subpart takes the test and expresses what he sees in the inkblots, wouldn't that be a way of determining the psychological and emotional state of that subpersonality? How many component elements would be exposed as a result of the test? What indeed could we discover about the protector or the controller? OK, let's take one of the child archetypes: the magical child subpart takes the test; what do we hear from that subpart and how is it so different from the protector? Then we try another of the child energies, the vulnerable child, and what is the difference in what each of the child archetypes sees? Certainly they would have very different responses that possibly would contain a variety of energies indigenous to them. I am not suggesting that every time an actor uses subpersonality as a choice approach to address an obligation in a scene he take an inkblot test; I am just using those examples to make an important point about the facets that exist in every subpersonality. Essentially I want every actor reading this to ask questions about what he experiences when inhabited by one of his other selves. This entire example of using the Rorschach test was hypothetically musing about "what ifs," to make the point that, if possible, it would be a very specific way to understand the variables in each subpersonality.

So far we are dealing with theories. What about the practical ways to discover what facets each of our subparts contains? And is it constant or does it change? If you, the actor, are experienced with subpersonality work and have been involved with it for some time, you can *roleplay* yourself into a subpart and actually determine how that energy feels and how many emotional elements you experience while you are inhabited by it. This is a moment when the eleventh level of consciousness should come into play. It stands above what you are experiencing and can objectively interpret the content of the experience and creatively manipulate it into the desired expressive area.

Another way to explore and discover the total contents of being inhabited by a subpart is voice dialogue. Having someone facilitate you would give you and the facilitator immediate knowledge of who is there and what energies are present in the facilitation. An additional advantage of voice dialogue is that the facilitator, after recognizing other components in the expression of the subpart, can creatively manipulate it into emphasizing the desired facet to take the forefront experientially.

EXAMPLE OF A VOICE-DIALOGUE SESSION

The facilitation starts with the facilitator sitting facing the person (actor) being facilitated. In this example both of them decide to explore the *inner-critic* subpersonality for the purpose of discovering what additional facets it might have.

FACILITATOR. Hi, how do you feel?

ACTOR. I am kind of excited to find out about this whole theory of facets.

FACILITATOR. OK, I'm just going to see who is there in the moment, and I don't want to go right to the inner critic. Is that OK with you?

ACTOR. Yes, that's OK.

FACILITATOR. What are you feeling right now?

ACTOR. I feel a little anxious, and I feel that I am anticipating getting into my inner critic, but I have positive feelings about you and I trust you.

FACILITATOR. OK, so when do you feel critical of yourself—I mean when is that part of you most present in your life?

ACTOR. He's there most of the time. He talks into my right ear telling me that I'm not doing something the way it should be done—things like that.

FACILITATOR. OK, move over a couple of feet to your right *(he does)*, and let me speak to him.

INNER CRITIC. *(After having found a comfortable place to stand.)* Yeah, OK, what do you want to know? How much of a loser he is? I'm sick of trying to get him to be responsible; it's exhausting!

FACILITATOR. What do you mean *responsible?*

INNER CRITIC. He's lazy; he wants everyone else in his life to do for him! He doesn't listen to me; I'm just about done with him.

FACILITATOR. I'm hearing in your voice that you are really angry. Is that right?

INNER CRITIC. Angry? I hate him, and I'm pissed and angry at his whole fucking family too! You have no idea how hard I have worked to reach him and his goddamn family!

(At this point the facilitator is hearing an angry and volatile voice coming from the inner critic. Ordinarily in a *conventional facilitation* he would ask to speak to that angry voice and any other voices that have just expressed themselves; however, for the purpose of exploring the potential of those energies coming from another facet of the inner critic, he continues facilitating the inner critic.)

FACILITATOR. So you hate him and are angry at him for being lazy and unresponsive to you. Is that correct?

INNER CRITIC. Yes, after a while I just gave up on him! Fuck him! I don't care what the hell he does!

FACILITATOR. You seem critical, angry, and I'm getting the feeling from you that you feel unappreciated about a lot of things and by a lot of people too.

INNER CRITIC. Yeah, that's right; you got it. Have you looked at the condition the world is in right now? It's fucked! Everybody is fucked up!

At this point in the facilitation it is quite apparent that there are a number of energies coming from the inner critic. Again, ordinarily in a conventional facilitation, the facilitator would interrupt and ask to speak to those other voices, but because of the emphasis of this facilitation, we are concentrating on learning about how many other elements (or energies) are contained in a single subpersonality. So does it mean that other subparts intruded and we are experiencing other subpersonalities, or does it mean that all of those energies are facets of the inner critic?

Determining whether the combination of those other voices or energies are other subparts that want to be heard or all part of the inner critic is something that the actor must explore, and maybe he will not be able to get a specific answer to that question. It doesn't matter though, because he can learn more about how each of his subpersonalities functions, and with the help of the *eleventh level of consciousness* he will be able to take advantage of all of his discoveries.

In the example of facilitating the actor's inner critic it became obvious that there were three different energies expressed during the facilitation: the critical element of the inner critic, the angry and frustrated energy, and an injustice-collector element.

How can the actor use and profit from the experience? What is there to learn about that specific subpart? There are three things he can do to make it very clear: First, roleplay himself into the inner critic, and once he is inhabited by the energy, ask him to talk, to do a sharing monologue. What he says will hopefully contain all the facets expressed during the facilitation.

Secondly, use the experience of the voice-dialogue facilitation to identify the various voices that intrude. The actor hears those voices and is now aware that they are not just the expected expression of how we think about what an inner critic does or sounds like. And he can discuss it with the facilitator and get some input from him. He now has more information about the behavior of the inner critic.

And in the third instance, he can use any one of the approach techniques for accessing subpersonalities to elicit the inner critic and again ask it to express itself verbally. The more you learn, the more you know about all of your subpersonalities.

There is also the impact that the specific content of a scene has on the subpersonality that the actor is using in it. A lot depends on the stimulus and the impetus that the material is supplying; for example, if the actor is into an intense confrontation with another character in the scene, that confrontation is going to have an effect on the subpart, and whatever that effect is, it will probably access a specific facet of the sub-personality inhabiting the actor.

All of the work we do as actors and all of the training that should go on for our entire lives are aimed at growing and evolving as artists. One of my personal gifts is that from early childhood I was curious about everything, so I asked questions: Why? How? When? How come? Much to the chagrin of parents, teachers or anyone doing anything that I wanted to know about! So to all of my fellow actors I say, Ask questions, ask questions and never stop asking. What don't we know if we don't know what we don't know? Well, let's find out.

TRAPPED IN SUBPERSONALITIES

Many people spend their entire lives trapped in one or more subpersonalities. It is acceptable to them because that is who they think they are. Without awareness or the establishment of an aware ego nothing changes. I have known people that have spent their whole adult life working seven days a week. They never took a vacation. You might say, Well, they enjoyed working. Maybe they did, but their lives certainly lacked any other selves that enjoyed other things. A person I knew was very responsible: He had a family, a wife whom he loved and four children. So one of his subpersonalities was the responsible self/father and the other was the workaholic. There was a certain satisfaction, I'm sure, in being able to take care of his family, but he was living a one-dimensional life! Not everyone is obligated or destined to make an important contribution to the world, but what about experiencing life on a multidimensional level? I also know a woman who has lived sixty-nine years as an unhappy spinster with not one friend in her life. So what was her story? At a much earlier time in her life she was influenced by a very disturbed and possessive mother, who spent many years convincing her that the world was an awful place filled with evil people who wanted to take advantage and hurt her. She was told that men only wanted to use women for sex and nothing else. So she became an injustice collector and lived mostly in her victim energy. I'm sure that she is still trapped in those subparts. Abusers are usually people who suffered abuse, so they became abusers. So many people grow up with so much pain and deprivation that they become trapped in a vengeful subpart that impels them to get even with the people in their world. People get trapped in a plethora of subpersonalities and quite often spend their lives in that box. For our purposes as actors, we should become aware of the multitude of characters in dramatic material that are trapped in one or more subpersonalities. When you identify a character in a play or film that behaves as if trapped in an identifiable subpart, it makes it clear what choices you can make to address that character.

Let's take for example the leading character in a film who is obsessed with achieving the fulfillment of all of his desires at the cost of everyone in his life. He has a blatant disregard for the lives of the people he knows and all the people in the world for that matter.

That is the description of a sociopath, so I think the major subpersonality would be the narcissist subpart, and the other subs would be the achiever and the pusher. So how do you, as the actor, approach this role in order to fulfill it organically? Since I have read and been told by a number of psychologists that narcissism is an incurable disease, then how would you approach the role using subpersonalities? Would you find a way to access narcissism as a choice? It is a good question. It is entirely possible to explore an ego state that resembles narcissism if you selectively emphasize creating an egoistic state and stay there for the duration of the performance. At any rate becoming aware of how people get trapped in a variety of subpersonalities gives the actor another tool for addressing characters who are being impelled by a subpart.

Near the end of 1955 I was in the army and was stationed at Fort Ord on the Monterey peninsula. I did the lead in a play at the Wharf Theater in Monterey, California. The play was *Night Must Fall,* written by an English actor and playwright, Emlyn Williams. I played a Cockney serial killer who preyed on older women. Danny, the character, would seek employment as a caretaker for rich older women and after ingratiating himself would kill them. He carried the heads of his victims around in a hatbox. It was a great role and the first time I played a serial killer. At that time in my life and training I did not have a solid craft and of course knew nothing about subpersonalities, so my acting was predicated on talent, instinct and intellect. I did some research on every character I played and would create a background for each of them. The background was either supplied by the author of the piece, or I would create it from imagination and fantasy. I imagined that Danny hated his mother, who had most likely abused him, and that killing these women was his way of killing his mother over and over! I really don't remember any more about how I created the character. I did, however, receive great praise about my performance. In retrospect Danny was obsessively trapped in several subpersonalities: *the angry, rebellious child, the victim* and *the killer-revenger energies.*

Remembering my experience set me off on a journey to research serial killers down through the ages. They have been around for centuries. Here is a list of some of the most famous recent ones:

Ted Bundy, John Wayne Gacy, Jeffrey Dahmer, Aileen Wuornos, Jack the Ripper, Albert Fish, Pedro Lopez, The Son of Sam (who was David Berkowitz), the Zodiac Killer and so many more. The strange thing is that people are fascinated by them. Many movies have been made about them. Jack the Ripper, for example, has been memorialized in more than half a dozen films, some of which I have seen over the years. Let's take him as an example of a killer who was trapped in subpersonalities: He almost exclusively killed prostitutes, dissected them with the skill of a surgeon. So why did he select prostitutes as his victims? Let's conjecture about his obsession: He had a very powerful moralist subpart, a *Martin Luther* subpersonality and an avenger-killer subpart that drove him to "rid the world" of those disgusting creatures that were polluting society. As far as is known he was never caught.

Aileen Wuornos was a prostitute and killed a lot of men. A movie was made about her, and Charlize Theron won the Academy Award for her portrayal of her. So what were the subpersonalities impelling her to kill so many people? Certainly an *injustice collector,* a *victim* and a *revenger* subpart. And I believe her sexual subpart was expressed homosexually because of her hatred for men.

The difference between a serial killer being trapped in various subpersonalities and normal people is that the serial killer is a psychopath. So what is a psychopath? Here is the Internet definition of sociopath and psychopath: "These are pop psychology terms for what psychiatry calls antisocial personality disorder. It is a mental disorder in which a person consistently shows no regard for right and wrong and ignores the rights and feelings of others. He or she shows no guilt or remorse for his or her behavior. A psychopath has no conscience, no remorse and no empathy for others. He or she is driven to fulfill his or her own needs and desires."

I could go through all of the above serial killers and conjecture about what subpersonalities they were trapped in. Some of the ones I researched had killed as many as three hundred people!

The reality is that, in my opinion, they were all trapped in some kind of obsessive subpart and had no awareness of those energies, while the rest of people (actors) that may be trapped in a subpart or several subparts need to develop an aware ego so that they can move on.

This section can be valuable for actors who may in their career play serial killers or are in a play or film where they have to deal with a character like that. As I said earlier, almost every one of the serial killers I mentioned had one or more movies made about them.

A subpersonality is created in an individual as a result of some event or experience that has a strong impact on him, often a traumatic experience or event. Since many of our subpersonalities develop to protect us, any threatening event will produce someone who comes into our lives to protect and control the situation. Some events are so traumatic and damaging that the protective subpersonality that is formed assumes a rigid hold on the person. Quite often that energy is so determined to protect that it pushes any other subpart that may present a threat deep into the disowned sphere, while at the same time it refuses to become aware of what it is doing.

Multiple-personality disorder or, as it is called now, dissociative identity disorder (DID) is characterized by the presence of two or more distinct identities. Each may have a unique name, personal history and individual characteristics. None of them are aware of each other. There are treatments, but the condition is incurable. The causes are not too clear, but many psychiatrists think it may have its origin in childhood traumas.

Those separate identities are total "other selves" with a distinct personality and individual characteristics that are indigenous to them and separate from each other. This is an extreme case where there is no consciousness or awareness present, so that none of the subpersonalities can do or be anything other than who they are.

I am including this to make a very important point. If there was any doubt in anyone's mind that subpersonalities really exist and that they are fully developed *people* that inhabit us, this should allay those doubts.

In the introduction to this book I said that I was going to demystify subpersonalities as a technique that actors can use to address dramatic material without thinking that there is some kind of a supernatural *woogie* thing about the process. Subpersonalities historically have been a psychological and consciousness tool, and they are all of that, and now in this book, they are an acting tool.

BONDING

This is a phenomenon that naturally takes place with subpersonalities. Our primary-self structure develops from birth to protect the vulnerable-child subpersonality and thus make sure that the child is safe. Many of the subpersonalities I listed earlier continue to evolve as the child grows. The protector-controller energies are extremely important in handling experiences that come up for the individual, and so are the inner critic, the pleaser, the pusher, the perfectionist, and so on. At the same time a group of opposite subpersonalities is relegated to the disowned-subpersonality structure. The primary selves are very intimidated by the disowned selves and work to keep them from manifesting themselves in the life of the person. Because of that division between the selves, a syndrome occurs, which is quite serious and can be very destructive to many people. A person who lives in his primary selves and is in denial of his disowned ones is destined to attract people into his life that are holding those disowned energies. I know it sounds a little strange, and when I first started working with subpersonalities, I was dubious as to the validity of that concept. In time, however, I experienced the veracity of this phenomenon and saw how in my own life I was attracting people who were obviously functioning from a place that I had not embraced. Until I began to recognize what was happening, I continued to attract people who held my disowned energies and only brought me frustration. With help I then began to create the necessary balance for myself by inviting my own disowned energies into my life. At first, it was a slow process of recognizing those opposite or disowned parts and accepting them by assuring my primary selves that it was safe to do so. In voice dialogue those primary subpersonalities were able to express their fears, and with further facilitation I was able to convince them that allowing the disowned selves to be recognized made them, the primaries, more secure and allowed me to balance the two sides. When I felt safe and became conscious of this process, I began to identify the splits in others—a powerful tool in dealing with them. Not only did it simplify my life, but it also made it possible for me to work with people in terms of the problems that were created by the bonding patterns they were experiencing.

RELATIONSHIPS

Again, we naturally attract into our life people who hold our disowned subpersonalities. We get involved in marriage or long-term relationships with them in total ignorance of the dynamics involved. Thousands of people are trapped in those unhappy marriages and relationships, and they stay there for years, unfulfilled and frustrated. The divorce rate is enormous, while other people bite the bullet and stay together for the children or for religious and financial reasons. They look for other people to get involved with, hoping that they will find in another person what is missing in their relationship, only to discover that almost always the dynamic repeats itself in the next encounter. The reasons they come up with to explain their boredom and disinterest is that familiarity has set in and the same old, same old behaviors keep being repeated. Sex becomes predictable, uninteresting and unfulfilling. They lose interest in each other's involvements and needs and find little to talk about. The real issue is that they really do not know what the problem is. They are totally without awareness of their bonding pattern.

If we become conscious of that pattern, the universe has given us the opportunity to learn from it and to reclaim ownership of our disowned subparts, which will give us the chance to address and solve the problems of a dysfunctional relationship and to breathe new and exciting life into what appears to have no exit from a place where both people are not conscious of what brought them together in the first place.

Example

Sheila is a very vulnerable young woman, who has always been in touch with her spiritual energy. She is expressive and is able to relate to others from a personal place. She was attracted to Adam, and after a brief courtship, they got married.

Adam is not in touch with his vulnerability and is in fact embarrassed by people who express vulnerable emotions. Unlike Sheila, he is very impersonal when relating to her and to others. What attracted them to each other is that they hold each other's disowned energies. Besides the fact that the original attraction was probably physical and sexual, the real magnetism came from disowned subparts. Almost from the onset, they were constantly in a state of conflict. Adam was put off by her vulnerability and criticized her "airy spirituality," and she was constantly frustrated by his cold and remote behavior. They fruitlessly kept on attempting to get from each other what they disowned in themselves. The problem was that they were totally unaware of what was really happening and could have gone on for years without any personal fulfillment in their relationship. The solution was to become conscious of their disowned subparts and, with help, to embrace those energies and create an aware ego related to the bonding pattern that they were in. With the help of a professional voice-dialogue facilitator they would eventually break out of that bonding pattern. Becoming conscious of the existence of those disowned energies is a great opportunity to redeem them. It is an incredible lesson that totally justifies their attraction to each other. Adam can embrace his sensitive and vulnerable subpersonality and experience a richer and more meaningful life, and at the same time Sheila will embrace a more focused and direct ability to be impersonal at those times when it is necessary for her to be able to fulfill functional obligations that her vulnerable self obstructed. And if they embrace their disowned selves, their relationship will be successfully fulfilling.

Thousands of people are in similar situations and find their way into psychotherapy hoping to change each other's personality and blaming each other for the problems. Consciousness may be the answer to saving a relationship and maybe the world.

When one becomes an experiential actor, there can be no separation between living and acting. In order to be able to experience what the character is experiencing, the actor must be liberated from all of the obstacles and blocks that he has in order to be free to act. Freeing yourself from the split between your primary-subpersonality structure and your disowned selves is necessary to achieving objectivity in your interpretation of the characters that you will address. That is not to say that you must embark on a journey to discover and identify your own issues in this area, but it is important to become aware of what parts of yourself are involved when you identify a bonding pattern in the two characters in the play that you have chosen to deal with. I have already discussed creating a subpersonality inventory to identify who is there on a daily basis. So it is important to listen to the voices that come to you when experiencing your daily involvements.

EXAMPLES OF BONDING PATTERNS IN CHARACTERS IN PLAYS AND FILMS

Martha and George in *Who's Afraid of Virginia Woolf* are definitely stuck in a bonding pattern. So much of their ongoing conflict is related to their disowned selves. The opposites are totally frustrating as both people struggle to get from one another what they disown in themselves. Martha is ambitious and aggressive, wants visibility and success in her life, and is constantly in conflict with George's vulnerability and lack of ambition. His lack of energy and his failure to want to move upward in life are constantly frustrating to both of them. There are other issues in the relationship that come into play, but the basic bonding pattern is what sustains the conflict and unhappiness in their relationship.

If the actor playing either of those roles starts with an exploration of the bonding issues and works to create them, it will lead to stimulating the emotional life and conflict between them. Of course, both actors should agree to work for the elements of the bonding pattern in order to establish it as the basis of their relationship. It is also possible to work it alone: Let's suppose that you are going to play George and you can access a subpart that stimulates the component energies of George's disowned selves organically, then wouldn't it be possible just to respond to the way the other actor relates to you? Wouldn't you feel the same way the character feels about the way the actress is attacking you?

The rehearsal process is more often used to block the scene or to solidify the actor's concepts than as it should be used—to explore, to experiment and to try various approaches to create the experiential realities of the character and his relationships with other characters.

Not all plays or films deal with characters who are bonded to each other; however, it is something every actor should consider when he reads a play. If there is a strong bonding pattern between two or more of the characters in the piece it will help the actor to make the right choices as he addresses the material.

Another example of a strong bonding issue between two characters is the play *Fool for Love*. Eddie and May are obsessed with each other and cannot be apart. Their sexual obsession with each other bonds them. However, they also have disowned elements in their sexual connection. Eddie looks for other liaisons and abandons May at times, while she seems to want and need a monogamous relationship. Therein are the disowned elements. If Eddie would embrace her needs and May would honor her disowned sexual energies, maybe they would come together and solve the conflict that they experience throughout the play. I am sure that Shepard was also dealing with other elements of their relationship. The fact that both of them had the same father created much of the complexity of their relationship.

In another Sam Shepard play, *True West,* the two brothers are in a strong bonded relationship. Austin, a Hollywood screenwriter, is well-educated and has a wife and children, while Lee, his older brother, is a drifter and a thief. There is a great contrast between them. Lee has never gone to college, but Austin is square and knows it. There is a lot of competition and jealousy coming from Lee, who is very aggressive towards Austin. Without going into a complete description of the play, I would say that the issue of bonding is quite obvious. Lee is brash and aggressively threatening, while Austin is intimidated by Lee and fears him. The opposites are very obvious. At some point later in the play they admit to being envious of each other's lives. Whether they embrace the existence of their disowned selves is questionable, however. The recognition of the divide would certainly take them into embracing those disowned energies. The actor playing either of the roles would be aided by acknowledging the bonding patterns in the characters.

Another film where there is a strong bonding issue between the characters is *The African Queen*, a film directed by John Huston and starring Humphrey Bogart and Katharine Hepburn. A dissolute steamer captain (Humphrey Bogart) offers a religious spinster safe passage after her brother is killed in West Africa. She is furious that her brother was killed by the Germans, and she persuades the Bogart character to destroy a German gunboat. The two of them spend most of their time fighting with each other rather than with the Germans; yet their time alone on the river leads to their falling in love with each other. They are totally opposite in their personalities, and it is obvious that they are both in denial of their disowned energies. He is sloppy, unkempt and antisocial in his language and behavior, while she couldn't be more proper and socially aware. As the action proceeds, however, they both begin to accept their differences and to recognize their disowned subparts.

Here is a list of films that contain characters who are in conflict because of disowned subpersonalities:

Gone with the Wind, Double Indemnity, A Streetcar Named Desire, Butch Cassidy and the Sundance Kid, Platoon, Mutiny on the Bounty, My Fair Lady, a Place in the Sun, and *Anna and the King of Siam—* which was later made into the musical *The King and I.* Quite often the relationship conflict in a play or film becomes the core element there. The struggle of the main characters is sometimes the bonding issue between them that causes the conflict and action of the piece. Take for example the relationship between Stanley and Blanche in *A Streetcar Named Desire.* The meat of the play is their relationship and how it evolves. They are both carrying each other's disowned selves, a problem that never gets resolved in the play.

There are many more plays and films where the conflict between the characters is driven by the existence of disowned subpersonalities. It is very important for you, the actor, reading this to understand that you might also have an issue in your life and your relationships that is complicated by the denial of your disowned selves. Becoming conscious of your own issues will make you much more capable of objectively identifying it in others and dealing with your craft.

HOW DO YOU DISCOVER YOUR DISOWNED SELVES?

There are three states of subpersonality awareness: Two that you know exist and the other, unconscious place that you are not in touch with—in other words, the *primary selves,* their opposites and the disowned subpersonalities that have been pushed deeply into the unconscious. Knowing specifically what the selves are in the primary structure will of course make you aware that there are subpersonalities that exist in opposite areas. With that knowledge it is easier to communicate with them and access them through voice dialogue and other techniques.

The third stage of subpersonality awareness is the disowned selves that have been pushed deeply into the unconscious and are much more difficult to access and address. The development of an *aware ego* is the goal in coming to terms with your ability to embrace and balance all of your selves. The bottom line is that the primary selves are frightened of the disowned sub-parts, thinking that they are there only to create havoc and injure you. Therefore your job is to become very educated about the dynamics and to work to assure the primary selves that the disowned selves will not harm the vulnerable-child energy.

If we knew what our disowned selves were, we would be able to avoid attracting the wrong people into our lives and having to do that dance. However, we are not usually gifted with that kind of awareness. A good way to start finding out about your disowned selves is to examine all of the relationships in your life. The ones that cause you the most frustration and angst are usually those that are holding your disowned energies. And you can fix them!

If you get involved with a facilitator and do voice dialogue for a period of time, your disowned selves will surface during the facilitation. When you become aware of them, you can include them in your life by embracing them and the primary selves equally.

Another way to find your disowned selves is to be very conscious of all of the subpersonalities in your primary-self structure. The more powerful and controlling a particular subpart is, the greater the fear and intimidation it has in relation to a disowned subpart. For example, let's say that a person has very powerful protector-controller energies; well, then, those subparts would not want the lazy beach-bum subpersonality to undermine the safety of the person! And the same mechanism would apply to all of the primary selves: the pusher, the inner critic, the perfectionist, the mind, and the wisdom voice.

Whom do you hate? Whom can't you tolerate? Who frustrates you beyond the beyond? The level of your distaste for another person is a strong indication that he or she holds one of your disowned selves. This holds true in so many ways. Comments such as, *He is so sloppy, unkempt; she doesn't care about anyone but herself; I have never known anyone so lazy; all he thinks about is sex; every other word out of his mouth is fucking or whom he would like to fuck; he hates anyone that is not like him or doesn't think like him,* are indications that a subpersonality is at play. As you become aware and willing to acknowledge those feelings, you will almost always find that they are sub-personalities that you have disowned.

Still another way to find disowned selves is in your dreams. They come to you and ask you for recognition and acceptance. In the next chapter I will go very deeply into the universe of dreams and dreaming. At the very moment you read this, you should begin to become aware of all your dreams.

CHAPTER 6

DREAMS AND DREAMING

Beginning this chapter of the book is like opening a door to another universe. There have been scores of books, papers, documentaries about the subject. It is a very important subject to me and my life. It has been an incredible journey with fabulous experiences and discoveries that have influenced and shaped my life for many decades. When you think about the fact that we sleep one third of our life away, you will realize that if you are fortunate enough to live to ninety, you will have slept for thirty years of your entire time on the planet. That is frightening, isn't it? The real tragedy is if you have not used those thirty years in a positive way. Dreaming is necessary for maintaining a healthy life, physically and mentally. Dreams are our greatest teachers, and besides what we learn from them, they are a source of adventure; they excite our imagination and help us find the right direction in life. I lost my son in 2006, but with the help of my dream life he is very much alive for me. Every time he visits me in my dreams, it is like having him there, and as long as I'm alive, he's still with me! With my involvement with subpersonalities, my dreams keep me in direct contact with who is there, who needs to be recognized, and what they are trying to communicate.

Even though the present emphasis on dreams and dreaming is to address the subject of this book, which is subpersonalities, I feel it is very necessary to instruct all of my readers as to all the mechanics of knowing and using dreams and to educate them as to the multifarious approaches to understanding, interpreting, learning and applying all of that knowledge to their advantage. In my book *Acting, Imaging and the Unconscious* I wrote a very specific section on dreams. It breaks down how to dream with great clarity, so I am going to plagiarize myself by borrowing some of that section from that book. I am going to amend and change some of the content to better serve the purposes of the subject matter and content of this book, however. In order to benefit from the dreams we have, we must understand the dream process and how to, with knowledge, analyze and use our dreams in an educated way.

The discussion, telling and analysis of dreams are an ancient involvement. Man has been addressing his dreams from the beginning of time. His religions, superstitions, and daily activities have been influenced and guided by his responses to them and his interpretation of their meaning. Only recently, however, has there been a scientific exploration of what, how and why we dream and what our dreams mean. C.G. Jung spearheaded it and wrote a great deal on the subject. He and Freud pioneered this incredible area, but hundreds of others have taken up the banner and made discoveries and contributions to it. Hundreds, possibly thousands of books and papers have been written about dreams, as well as infinite techniques and suggestions given for understanding, exploring, interpreting and learning from them. There are so many ways to relate to and use our dreams and so much to be gotten from becoming sophisticated about the dream process! If used properly, our dreams can help us antidote lifelong obstacles and inhibitions. They can teach us the lessons that the unconscious wishes to communicate and bring us a greater understanding of ourselves and the knowledge that will help us solve psychological and other problems. Unfortunately, they quite frequently lack continuity and can jump from one environment to another without any logical transition. They are also often rather abstract and filled with symbolism. Therefore, it takes some training or research to understand them and be able to use them creatively. As acting tools, dreams can serve us in a variety of important ways. They can also be used to identify the existence of DISOWNED SUBPERSONALITIES. And I will get to that later in this section and give you examples of dreams where it was clear that a disowned subpersonality was asking to be recognized. I also want to explore and emphasize dreams and dreaming as a way to create a connection with the unconscious and to seduce it into serving our creative needs.

STARTING THE PROCESS

So where do you begin this incredible journey? That, of course depends on where you are in the world of dreaming. If you are at the very beginning, you must start with DREAM AWARENESS. If you have been working and exploring your dreams for a period of time, the dream awareness section will be a good reminder. It outlines a systematic process for becoming aware of dreams and using them to build a bridge from consciousness to the unconscious.

DREAM AWARENESS

You would be surprised at the number of people who think that they never dream or at least that they do so very infrequently. We all dream every single night or whenever we sleep. We may have as many as ten or fifteen dreams in a single night. A number of them are quite subliminal and we don't remember having had them at all. There are some which we are aware of while we are sleeping, but they evaporate even before we experience the first glimmer of consciousness. Some of us remember our dreams for a very few moments after awakening, but they vanish so quickly that we only have a vague sense of having dreamed at all. Other people remember in great detail many of their dreams. There are many reasons for those personal differences. Certain people are just more closely connected with the conscious-unconscious process, and they also have lucid dreams, which I will discuss later in this chapter. Whatever the case may be for you, there is a process for remembering and using your dreams. **It starts with awareness**.

The first step is to accept that you dream every time you sleep and that you can remember those dreams long enough to record them. Planting that knowledge in your consciousness will start the process of expecting yourself to dream. Once you have done that, you must ask yourself to remember what you dream. Upon awakening, stay in bed, preferably in a prone position, and go over the events and elements of the dream, allowing yourself to feel the dream. Encourage a state of relaxation and, if possible, keep your eyes closed to avoid collision with the waking world and its distractions. Continue encouraging the state of not being fully awake and invite a sensorial connection to the dream. In addition to feeling the dream, try to experience the sounds and smells you encountered there, and allow the temperature of the place to affect you. Employ all of your senses! After doing that, quickly write the dream down. Keep a pad and pencil or a tape recorder by your bedside so that you can record the dream in detail to work with it later. The conscious habit of remembering and exploring your dreams in this manner will open that world up to you. This connection is a life-changing involvement, and there is no limit to how far you can travel on this journey. Many people who started on it became so involved in that universe that they spent their entire life pursuing and interpreting their dreams and becoming professionals in the field.

Once you are awake, and possibly at a later time, you may go back to your notes and begin to work with the dream. After you encourage an awareness of dreaming, the next step is to prepare to dream.

INVITING THE DREAM

Inviting yourself to dream and encouraging yourself to remember the dreams are conscious processes. There are many facets to this involvement. It starts with a very deliberate decision to have a dream or a number of dreams. As you get into bed, do any of the relaxation exercises indigenous to this work. Encourage a complete state of physical and mental relaxation. At a point when you are completely relaxed, tell yourself that you are going to dream tonight and that you will remember your dreams. Make the suggestion quite specific and firm: "Tonight I am going to dream! I will remember all of my dreams. I know that I dream every time I sleep, so I am inviting those dreams into my life." As you wake up, whether it is in the middle of the night or in the morning, stay with the dream and do everything to remember and record it. If you awaken in the middle of a dream and there is still some sleeping time remaining, try to reinvest in the dream. Tell yourself that you are going back to sleep and will pick up the dream wherever it left off. That doesn't always work, but sometimes it does. By doing that, you can possibly have a resolution to the dream—which may be very important to your sense of well-being for the rest of the day. In addition, each time you succeed in continuing the dream, you may be strengthening your connection to conscious-unconscious communication. Encourage yourself to dream every time you go to sleep. At first, you may only have little success with your request, but do it consistently. The rewards will be forthcoming. Try to remember, if you are just at the beginning of learning about dreams and dreaming, that the unconscious is not accustomed to taking orders! However, with repetition and encouragement, it will soon begin to cooperate.

DREAM CATCHING

Dream catching refers to the process of being aware of the dream—its parts and elements, the place, time, people, animals, and objects in it. Dream catching can occur while you are still asleep, if you become aware that you are dreaming, or when you wake up. If in those few moments when you can still remember the dream you note all its elements, you can use them for later reconstruction.

Besides feeling the dream, which not only means identifying the way it makes you feel but feeling into its fabric (dreams have a fabric, a quality, an essence that frequently cannot be described but can be felt), ask questions about it while you are still in the sleep state, such as, Where is this place? Am I familiar with it? Does it feel like my environment? Who are these people? Do I recognize them? Whom do they remind me of? What are they trying to tell me? What is the plot of this dream? You might even talk to the characters in the dream and ask them what they are trying to communicate, why they are there, what they want, why they are doing what they are doing, and so on. Wait for them to respond! This is a very special time, when you are close enough to your unconscious to actually get answers that may even be startling. Most often, the characters in your dreams are subjective, which mean that they represent parts of yourself, which indeed may be subpersonalities who need to be recognized, acknowledged and included in your life. Sometimes the characters are more objective—which means that they represent other people in your life—and the dream may be telling you something about them or your relationship to them that needs to be clarified or paid attention to. Catching the dream is extremely important for a variety of reasons: first, so that you might be able to understand the message, and secondly, so that you have enough components to re-create and work with the dream from a conscious place.

LUCID DREAMING

Simply put, lucid dreaming occurs when you are asleep and having a dream and you know that you are dreaming. It does not happen very often to most people, but when it does it is an astounding experience. You can become an observer of the dream experience or a participant. There are many theories about what causes lucid dreaming, even that it might be something you ate before going to bed! While in the midst of lucidity, any participation will usually not interrupt the dream. You can change the ingredients of the dream, taking it into another direction or completely changing its outcome.

So how in subpersonality terms can we put lucid dreaming to work for us? I have already talked about objective and subjective dreaming and the difference between the two. A subjective dream is a part of you talking and behaving a certain way in the dream. If the greatest benefit we derive from our dreams is what we learn from them, we should pay special attention to what the person (character) in the dream is asking for, what he is telling us that we should pay specific attention to. In the sections in my other books that are related to subpersonalities, there was an emphasis on the disowned subparts asking to be recognized and included in the dreamer's life. The primary selves are also vying for attention and recognition. Ask yourself, What are they saying? What are they asking of me? Is it possible in a lucid dream to have a two-way conversation with them? And if so, what can I learn from the encounter? Lucid dreaming is rare and only happens once in a great while. You can ask for a lucid dream just the way you would ordinarily invite a regular dream. Of course, there are no guarantees that it will happen. One of the ways to encourage it, and this is entirely unscientific, is to work with the hypnagogic state, which manifests itself normally just before you fall asleep or just as you are waking up. It happens very fast! It is the moment before consciousness gives way to the unconscious. You are no longer awake but not yet fully asleep. It is that point when the unconscious is communicating with the conscious part of you. In this state strange things come into your consciousness that are often bizarre and not understandable. If you can catch a wisp of them and hopefully understand any of it, it would be a gift of some worth. I personally have been working with it for a very long time now, and at first it was extremely frustrating because like smoke it evaporated so quickly. I started to work with what I call a "pre-hypnagogic state." Ordinarily it takes me some time to fall asleep, no matter how tired I may be, so I trained myself to be aware of the exact moment when I was nodding off and to stop myself from falling asleep to try to promote that sleep-wake moment. At times it worked for a few split moments and I was able to mine a few unconscious stimuli to enter my consciousness. When that does occur, and it has, it feels as though the messages, whatever they seem to be, are coming from another dimension outside of what we know. I cannot swear to having success in stimulating lucid dreaming, but I can say it seems to have created a stronger connection to my unconscious and has delivered some very impacting dreams. I really believe that doing this is a way to encourage the unconscious and the conscious states to mesh with each other. With continual practice I have experienced a greater connection in my dream life with pulling up much more stuff from the unconscious regions.

ACTIVE IMAGINATION

I would now like to introduce a technique created by Jung, called *active imagination.* Jung felt that it was an important way to consciously relate to the unconscious. You can start by talking to the people in your dreams, putting any of them in a chair facing you and starting a conversation. Ask questions such as, Who are you? What do you want here? Why are you behaving this way? What were you doing in my living room? Where did you come from? Allow the figure to answer. This is a highly imaginative process, and since it originates in the dream world, the answers you get may surprise you. You can use the process in relation to all of the characters in your dreams. You may even ask questions about the place or actions of the dream. Allow the characters to respond and tell you why they are appearing and what they want. They may be reluctant to cooperate with you and your query, and maybe you should not push them. Establishing a simple and benevolent attitude towards them will go a long way in getting them to be willing to communicate.

EXAMPLES OF REAL DREAMS

All of the dreams I will be using as examples are my own dreams, most of which I recorded daily for several months, from April 26 to July 15, 2018. I stopped doing it because it had taken over my life and kept me from living in the waking world. However, my work with dreams continues to the present day, and since I remember my dreams vividly I don't need to record them in the same way I used to. I created a code for myself that I use to recall a certain dream by using a keyword related to it. When I say that word, and it is usually one that relates to the content of the dream, it brings back the entire dream for me.

I do not believe in self-medication, but I believe in self-awareness. Using your dreams to address personal, physical and psychological issues is an important way to bring balance into your life. Understanding and using subpersonalities as an approach to achieving balance is the main purpose of learning from your other selves. I have had an anxiety issue for most of my life. I have been in psychotherapy on and off for more than thirty years, and while it has been of great help for me, working with subpersonalities for about the same period has also been extremely helpful in dealing with a variety of issues. In my last book, *A Second Chance at Life,* I spoke about using dreams to identify disowned selves as they appeared, asking to be recognized and accepted. In this section on dreams I am going to go deeper into using and understanding what our dreams are communicating to us.

Last night I had a dream, and without writing it down I remembered it:

I was with someone, who might have been my wife, I'm not sure. I was anxious about completing two more years of college since I had only finished two years. I needed to earn a bachelor's degree, and was troubled about going down to the school to register and choose next semester's classes. I complained about the parking issue. There were never enough parking spaces, and I also wasn't sure which building I needed to go to. It was confusing. I didn't seem to recognize which building was the right one, or whether I was actually in the right area to begin with. I felt my heart pounding and I was sweating. The feeling was easily recognized, since I have experienced it many times before. About that time the dream ended.

I woke up feeling anxious, and I was perspiring. I thought about the dream for some time, lying there in bed staring at the ceiling. Of course, I knew it was an anxiety dream, and like fear dreams this kind is also easy to interpret. Understanding anxiety is easy; where it comes from is not so easy!

I believe the dream was inspired by my anxiety about completing this book I am writing. Being in lockdown during the Covid-19 pandemic has afforded me time to write, which is frequently interrupted by my virtual-teaching responsibilities and often blocked by other responsibilities. And there is the "rub"! I am a very responsible person and have incredible discipline, which in this case is not an asset. My responsible sub-personality is overnourished and has been a priority for most of my life, which creates a disowning of the opposite subpart, the beach bum, the part that knows how to kick back and mellow out. In dealing with any issue such as anxiety you must explore the dynamics of what subpersonalities are in action.

In reality I have a couple of college degrees, which didn't occur to me in the dream.

A number of years ago, when I was working with Hal Stone in that group I shared a dream that I had:

I was taking care of a small fair-haired little boy about five years old. I was responsible for his welfare, and I took that responsibility seriously. I needed to be there for him at all times, and I was to make sure that he wanted for nothing. I knew who the little boy was and in spite of that knowledge I was committed to my job. He was Adolf Hitler as a child!

I shared that dream with Hal and everyone in the group. I was really disturbed by it, since I hate Hitler and the Nazis, who were responsible for killing my father's whole family in Russia. I was totally confused by the dream.

Hal listened and then interpreted it for me. He said that it was my own "dictator" subpersonality that was asking me to be recognized and accepted and embraced into my subpersonality structure.

At first I had difficulty in accepting that interpretation, but soon I understood that there was a justification for the dream. At that time in my life I was in a very difficult marriage and had difficulty saying NO or standing up for myself, taking charge, laying down the rules of our relationship. When I understood it, everything about the dream made sense to me.

Dream #3: I was in my car with a woman in the passenger seat. We were stuck behind a truck, and there was a bus right behind us. Smoke was coming from somewhere in front of the line of cars I was trapped behind. The smoke was very black and thick, and it was hard to breathe. I felt trapped and helpless and resigned to a terrible fate. That is where the dream ended.

I thought about it for a while and came up with an interpretation: in my primary-self structure I was most likely in either a helpless-child archetype or a helpless-adult energy. Why didn't we just get out of the car and find a way to walk to safety? There was definitely a disowned self that was asking to be included, the sub-part that is aggressive and takes action!

Dream #4: I was somewhere that looked like a school or public place, and Robert Redford was there signing autographs and being really kind to all of the people there. I was just watching, observing what was happening. I had no interaction with him. And then I was with him in a second place. We were talking, and I told him that I was an actor, and it was as if suddenly he recognized me as a member of his family, and I said, "Yes, I have been acting for a long time. Let me show you my résumé," and I started to look for it but couldn't find it. I told him that I had written eight books on acting and I wanted to give all of them to him. He said OK, but he had to leave for an appointment, and could I bring them to him tomorrow? I said, "Yes, of course," and that is where the dream ended.

I thought about that dream for several days. I was a little confused about it. What was it telling me? Am I star struck? Why Robert Redford? I have worked with and taught many successful actors, movie stars! So what was that dream telling me? After about a week I figured it out: I have lived with two mantras: stay hungry, keep reaching and never get self-impressed. I have honored those precepts all of my adult life and career. The dream was telling me that there was a part of me that was reaching out for recognition of my accomplishments, and that I was subordinating myself to the success and achievements of others and it was about time to claim my place in the world. So that too was a disowned subpersonality that was relegated to my other disowned selves. After recognizing the meaning of that dream I was able to embrace that subpart without changing my mantra.

Dream #5: I was on the telephone with my cousin Irving (background: we grew up together, we were in the Boy Scouts together, and we spent a lot of time sharing activities. He was twenty months older than I). He and his wife, Vera, are now deceased, but at that time they were in an assisted-living place in Indiana. His daughter Marla had told me that he did nothing but watch TV, eat and sleep. So in the dream I said to him on the phone, "Irving, you are not going to like what I am going to say to you, but please listen: You are just existing in that place waiting to die! If you don't get involved with living, that is what is going to happen sooner or later."

I had this dream in May 2018, and when I read it in the present I immediately understood that it was a subjective dream. I was really speaking to myself. I was eighty-six at the time of the dream and very much in touch with my mortality as I still am, and I have anxiety about being able to accomplish all that I wish to in the time that is left for me. And even if I wasn't in the same situation as my cousin Irving, the dream was telling me to be involved creatively in living. It was a subpersonality that was speaking to me in that dream, instructing me to use every minute of my life to my advantage.

Those are a few examples of my dreams that hopefully will communicate the importance of dreams and dreaming and how to use and understand them in relation to subpersonalities.

IN CONCLUSION

From the beginning of my involvement with sub-personalities, I used and modified the technique for actors to implement it as an acting tool. I have used it in my classes and as an approach when I was teaching and directing actors. I also wrote about subpersonalities as related to acting in three of my other books. They are one of the five megapproaches in my system.

Since Hal Stone ended up calling subpersonalities a consciousness-raising approach, and since my firm belief in my entire body of work is that there is no separation between living and acting, I can say that sub-personalities have a double impact on actors or people using it. Fifty percent of my work, my teaching, is related to liberating the instrument of actors so that they are free to act—eliminating obstacles, blocks, fear, tension, dependencies, emotional obstacles and life's damage. Subpersonality work is an incredible tool for elevating a person's awareness as to what is blocking and stopping him from being open and freely expressive. Of course, it is just one of a plethora of techniques, exercises and approaches that I have innovated to free the actor. It is, however, a very important one!

I know that in my introduction to this book I promised to demystify the process and make it much more people friendly. I believe that I have accomplished that; however, I am not so sure that I have made it less complex. New and different concepts and ideas challenge the precepts and specifics of the original approaches. Some of them stretch and expand subpersonalities as a living and acting approach. This book is specifically directed to actors and can also be profitable for directors.

I often remember an experience I had with the acting teacher that I was in partnership with, Curt Conway. Originally a successful actor on Broadway, he had been blacklisted during that HUAC, McCarthy period when they were looking for Communists under every rock, a shameful period in American history. It stopped his acting career, so he began teaching acting to survive. Anyway, this happened before I had written any books, when I told him that I was thinking about writing a book about acting, to which he responded in a very patronizing way, "What do you think you have to say about acting that has not already been said?" Well, ten books later, I think there is still more to say about acting!

The reason I shared that experience with you is that it is part of the meaningful points I wish to make about this book and you the reader. Many of the

exercises and techniques outlined here must be practiced and used on a daily basis. I know that with all of
the other exercises and techniques that an actor must
include in his daily workout schedule, as I said before,
he would need ten more hours to be added to each day.
Well, you must learn to prioritize what you should be
doing and when to do it, and then you will be able to
cover all of it. Remember, an actor is an actor twenty-
four hours a day, four weeks a month, twelve months a
year for life. And if you are not doing the work every
day, then achieving the ability to become an experiential actor would become remote.

In the foreword to my first book, *No Acting Please,*
Jack Nicholson wrote, "This work is not for everyone."
What did he mean when he said that? I believe he
meant that you have to decide what kind of actor you
want to be. So ask yourself right now as you read this,
stop and ask yourself, What kind of actor do I want to
be?

There are thirty-one choice approaches in my system, five of which are called megapproaches. I have
already explained what megapproaches are. However,
to elevate their importance I am going to use a metaphor: The other twenty-seven choice approaches are
part of our solar system, whereas subpersonalities and
the other megapproaches are part of another galaxy in
the universe! Subpersonality work is therapeutically
life changing as well as an incredible acting approach.

In conclusion, I want to make a special note here
of several of the meaningful changes and elements I
have added to the work. Some of them had not been

mentioned or explored before, but I described them in detail throughout this book.

The Eleventh Level of Consciousness

Pay attention to *the eleventh level of consciousness*, a very necessary tool when exploring subpersonalities, particularly when you are using some of the accessing techniques for inhabiting particular subparts, such as roleplaying. It is also very important if you get trapped in a subpart and are not conscious of how to get free of it. The eleventh level of consciousness works in concert with the aware ego.

Subpersonality Inventory

This is an assignment added to your responsibilities. You must do it every day, each time you shift from one mood to another, or when something happens that affects you, in order to know the dynamics of moving from one subpart to another. If you are not aware of those changes of energies, you can become a victim when a particular subpersonality moves into control of you. Establishing this awareness is not only emotionally healthy, but it can also be used to address an obligation related to a piece of material that you are working on. The inventory that you do on a daily basis also helps you to discover subpersonalities that you are not aware of.

Experience Hunting

I have been using choice hunting as an exercise in my classes for many years for the reasons I outlined earlier in this book. So for subpersonality purposes I modified the technique and called it experience hunting. When used for this purpose the emphasis is on discovering what, where, and when specific subpersonalities entered your life. What was the event, experience, or relationship element that created that other self? And how does it function in your life now?

Approach Techniques to Access Subpersonalities

I have listed ten accessing approaches, explaining how to use them and in what framework. Every one of the ten approaches is described in great detail.

Exploring the Multiple Facets of Each of Your Subpersonalities

This is probably the most important new aspect of the subpersonality process to date. It is something for which I have been doing an investigative exploration for some time now. I have not introduced it into my subpersonality jamborees or suggested it to people in my classes, and I have not written about it before now, because I have personally been experimenting with it in my own involvement, using it as an accessing technique to see how many different facets a subpart could have. Which facet is totally dependent on how it is elicited? What is the stimulus or impetus that calls the subpart forth, and how does that determine what the colors or facets look like and how they behave? Until now it has been understood that every subpersonality exists only to do what it is supposed to do. That means that the protector-controller only protects and controls, the pleaser pleases, the Don Juan sexual subpart is just the male sexual energy and so on. It is a simplistic and limiting concept of what each subpersonality does. Up until now the thought was that if there were other facets to a subpart it meant that another energy or another subpersonality was breaking in or moving into the forefront. And for decades that is what the accepted definition of those changes was. In voice-dialogue facilitation, the facilitator would often recognize emotional changes or different energies being expressed, and at that point he would say, "I hear another voice; would you move over and let me talk to that part?" There are a multitude of stimuli and circumstances that determine accessing the various facets of a subpart. The actor must become conscious and aware of those separate facets and know how to access and deal with a subpersonality that is elicited by a certain stimulus. It is more specifically explored within the content of the book. I just thought it might be important to give you a heads up about how important this element is in working with your other selves.

I hope that you will get a lot from this book and will be open to including all the added elements suggested herein. The book is not to be addressed as a novel, and you may have to reread many of the sections repeatedly so as to solidify your understanding and use of all of those techniques and concepts. Don't be afraid to challenge anything, but be willing to have an open mind and explore.

BIBLIOGRAPHY

Dyak, Miriam. *The Voice Dialogue Facilitator's Manual.* L I F E Energy Pr. 1st edition, 1999.

Jung, Carl G. "Approaching the Unconscious." in *Man and His Symbols,* edited by Carl G. Jung. 5th ptg. edition. Aldus Books, Limited. London, 1971.

Jung, Carl G. *The Archetypes and the Collective Unconscious,* 2nd ed. Bollingen Series XX. Princeton, NJ: Princeton University Press, 1968.

Natterson, Joseph. *The Dream in Clinical Practice.* Jason Aronson Inc. 1995.

Newmark, Amy and Kelly Sullivan Walden. *Chicken Soup for the Soul: Dreams and the Unexplainable.* Chicken Soup for the Soul, LLC. 2017.

Rowan, John. *Subpersonalities: The People inside Us. Routledge, 1990.*

Stone, Hal and Sidra Stone. *Embracing Our Selves,* new edition, Nataraj Publishing. 1989.

—— *Embracing Each Other.* Delos, Inc. 1989.

—— *Embracing Your Inner Critic.* San Francisco: Harper Collins, 1993.

—— *Partnering: A New Kind of Relationship.* Nataraj Publishing. 2000.

Walden, Kelly Sullivan. *It's All in Your Dreams. Conari Press. 2013*

NOTES